Principles
in Practice

D1320583

The Principles in Practice imprint offers teachers concrete illustrations of effective classroom practices based in NCTE research briefs and policy statements. Each book discusses the research on a specific topic, links the research to an NCTE brief or policy statement, and then demonstrates how those principles come alive in practice: by showcasing actual classroom practices that demonstrate the policies in action; by talking about research in practical, teacher-friendly language; and by offering teachers possibilities for rethinking their own practices in light of the ideas presented in the books. Books within the imprint are grouped in strands, each strand focused on a significant topic of interest.

Volumes in the Adolescent Literacy Strand

Adolescent Literacy and the Teaching of Reading
Lessons for Teachers of Literature

Deborah Appleman
Carleton College

National Council of Teachers of English
1111 W. Kenyon Road, Urbana, Illinois 61801-1096

Staff Editor: Carol Roehm

Imprint Editor: Cathy Fleischer

Interior Design: Victoria Pohlmann

Cover Design: Pat Mayer

Cover Image: Thompson-McClellan Photography

NCTE Stock Number: 00561

Library of Congress Cataloging-in-Publication Data

Appleman, Deborah.
   Adolescent literacy and the teaching of reading : lessons learned from a teacher of literature / Deborah Appleman.
        p. cm.
   Includes biliographical references and index.
   ISBN 978-0-8141-0056-1 ((pbk : alk. paper)
  1. Reading (Secondary) 2. Literature—Study and teaching (Secondary) 3. Teenagers —Books and reading. I. Title.
   LB1632.A67 2010
   428.4071'2—dc22

                                                                          2010014346

For all my students, for all that you have taught me

Contents

Acknowledgments

Many, many thanks to Cathy Fleischer, whose vision, perseverance, and skill have made this series a reality.

Thanks, too, to all my colleagues in the field of literacy education whose work continues to inspire me. You know who you are.

Thanks to Krista Herbstrith for her expert assistance with the manuscript.

Finally, thanks to John Schmit, without whom, nothing, including the writing of this book, would be possible.

Adolescent Literacy
An NCTE Policy Research Brief

Causes for Concern

It is easy to summon the language of crisis in discussing adolescent literacy. After all, a recent study of writing instruction reveals that 40 percent of high school seniors never or rarely write a paper of three or more pages, and although 4th and 8th graders showed some improvement in writing between 1998 and 2002, the scores of 12th graders showed no significant change. Less than half of the 2005 ACT-tested high school graduates demonstrated readiness for college-level reading, and the 2005 National Assessment of Educational Progress (NAEP) reading scores for 12th graders showed a decrease from 80 percent at the *proficient* level in 1992 to 73 percent in 2005.

Recent NAEP results also reveal a persistent achievement gap between the reading and writing scores of whites and students of color in 8th and 12th grades. Furthermore, both whites and students of color scored lower in reading in 2005 as compared with 1992, and both male and female students also scored lower in 2005.[1]

The challenges associated with adolescent literacy extend beyond secondary school to both college and elementary school. Many elementary school teachers worry about the 4th-grade slump in reading abilities. Furthermore, preliminary analysis of reading instruction in the elementary school suggests that an emphasis on processes of how to read can crowd out attention to reading for ideas, information, and concepts—the very skills adolescents need to succeed in secondary school. In the other direction, college instructors claim that students arrive in their classes ill-prepared to take up the literacy tasks of higher education, and employers lament the inadequate literacy skills of young workers. In our increasingly "flat" world, the U.S. share of the global college-educated workforce has fallen from 30 percent to 14 percent in recent decades as young workers in developing nations demonstrate employer-satisfying proficiency in literacy.[2]

In this context, many individuals and groups, including elected officials, governmental entities, foundations, and media outlets—some with little knowledge of the field—have stepped forward to shape policies that impact literacy instruction. Notably, the U.S. Congress is currently discussing new Striving Readers legislation (Bills S958 and HR2289) designed to improve the literacy skills of middle and high school students. Test scores and other numbers do not convey the full complexity of literacy even though they are effective in eliciting a feeling of crisis. Accordingly, a useful alternative would be for teachers and other informed professionals to take an interest in policy that shapes literacy instruction. This document provides research-based information to support that interest.

Common Myths about Adolescent Literacy

Myth: Literacy refers only to reading.

Reality: Literacy encompasses reading, writing, and a variety of social and intellectual practices that call upon the voice as well as the eye and hand. It also extends to new media—including nondigitized multimedia, digitized multimedia, and hypertext or hypermedia.[3]

Adolescent Literacy

Myth: Students learn everything about reading and writing in elementary school.

Reality: Some people see the processes of learning to read and write as similar to learning to ride a bicycle, as a set of skills that do not need further development once they have been achieved. Actually literacy learning is an ongoing and nonhierarchical process. Unlike math where one principle builds on another, literacy learning is recursive and requires continuing development and practice.[4]

Myth: Literacy instruction is the responsibility of English teachers alone.

Reality: Each academic content area poses its own literacy challenges in terms of vocabulary, concepts, and topics. Accordingly, adolescents in secondary school classes need explicit instruction in the literacies of each discipline as well as the actual content of the course so that they can become successful readers and writers in all subject areas.[5]

Myth: Academics are all that matter in literacy learning.

Reality: Research shows that out-of-school literacies play a very important role in literacy learning, and teachers can draw on these skills to foster learning in school. Adolescents rely on literacy in their identity development, using reading and writing to define themselves as persons. The discourses of specific disciplines and social/cultural contexts created by school classrooms shape the literacy learning of adolescents, especially when these discourses are different and conflicting.[6]

Myth: Students who struggle with one literacy will have difficulty with all literacies.

Reality: Even casual observation shows that students who struggle with reading a physics text may be excellent readers of poetry; the student who has difficulty with word problems in math may be very comfortable with historical narratives. More important, many of the literacies of adolescents are largely invisible in the classroom. Research on reading and writing beyond the classroom shows that students often have literacy skills that are not made evident in the classroom unless teachers make special efforts to include them.[7]

Myth: School writing is essentially an assessment tool that enables students to show what they have learned.

Reality: While it is true that writing is often central to assessment of what students have learned in school, it is also a means by which students learn and develop. Research shows that informal writing to learn can help increase student learning of content material, and it can even improve the summative writing in which students show what they have learned.[8]

Understanding Adolescent Literacy

Overview: Dimensions of Adolescent Literacy

In adolescence, students simultaneously begin to develop important literacy resources and experience unique literacy challenges. By fourth grade many students have learned a number of the basic processes of reading and writing; however, they still need to master literacy practices unique to different levels, disciplines, texts, and situations. As adolescents experience the shift to content-area learning, they need help from teachers to develop the confidence and skills necessary for specialized academic literacies.

Adolescents also begin to develop new literacy resources and participate in multiple discourse communities in and out of school. Frequently students' extracurricular literacy proficiencies are not valued in school. Literacy's link to community and identity means that it can be a site of resistance for adolescents. When students are not recognized for bringing valuable, multiple-literacy practices to school, they can become resistant to school-based literacy.[9]

1. Shifting Literacy Demands

The move from elementary to secondary school entails many changes including fundamental ones in the nature of literacy requirements. For adolescents, school-based literacy shifts as students engage with disciplinary content and a wide variety of difficult texts and writing tasks. Elementary school usually prepares students in the processes of reading, but many adolescents do not understand the multiple dimensions of content-based literacies. Adolescents may struggle with reading in some areas and do quite well with others. They may also be challenged to write in ways that conform to new disciplinary discourses. The proliferation of high-stakes tests can complicate the literacy learning of adolescents, particularly if test preparation takes priority over content-specific literacy instruction across the disciplines.[10]

Research says . . .

- Adolescents are less likely to struggle when subject area teachers make the reading and writing approaches in a given content area clear and visible.
- Writing prompts in which students reflect on their current understandings, questions, and learning processes help to improve content-area learning.[11]
- Effective teachers model how they access specific content-area texts.
- Learning the literacies of a given discipline can help adolescents negotiate multiple, complex discourses and recognize that texts can mean different things in different contexts.
- Efficacious teaching of cross-disciplinary literacies has a social justice dimension as well as an intellectual one.[12]

2. Multiple and Social Literacies

Adolescent literacy is social, drawing from various discourse communities in and out of school. Adolescents already have access to many different discourses including those of ethnic, online, and popular culture communities. They regularly use literacies for social and political purposes as they create meanings and participate in shaping their immediate environments.[13]

Teachers often devalue, ignore, or censor adolescents' extracurricular literacies, assuming that these literacies are morally suspect, raise controversial issues, or distract adolescents

Adolescent Literacy

from more important work. This means that some adolescents' literacy abilities remain largely invisible in the classroom.[14]

Research says . . .

- The literacies adolescents bring to school are valuable resources, but they should not be reduced to stereotypical assumptions about predictable responses from specific populations of students.
- Adolescents are successful when they understand that texts are written in social settings and for social purposes.
- Adolescents need bridges between everyday literacy practices and classroom communities, including online, non-book-based communities.
- Effective teachers understand the importance of adolescents finding enjoyable texts and don't always try to shift students to "better" books.[15]

 3. Importance of Motivation

Motivation can determine whether adolescents engage with or disengage from literacy learning. If they are not engaged, adolescents with strong literacy skills may choose not to read or write. The number of students who are not engaged with or motivated by school learning grows at every grade level, reaching epidemic proportions in high school. At the secondary level, students need to build confidence to meet new literacy challenges because confident readers are more likely to be engaged. Engagement is encouraged through meaningful connections.[16]

Research says . . .

Engaged adolescents demonstrate internal motivation, self-efficacy, and a desire for mastery. Providing student choice and responsive classroom environments with connections to "real life" experiences helps adolescents build confidence and stay engaged.[17]

A. Student Choice

- Self-selection and variety engage students by enabling ownership in literacy activities.
- In adolescence, book selection options increase dramatically, and successful readers need to learn to choose texts they enjoy. If they can't identify pleasurable books, adolescents often lose interest in reading.
- Allowing student choice in writing tasks and genres can improve motivation. At the same time, writing choice must be balanced with a recognition that adolescents also need to learn the literacy practices that will support academic success.
- Choice should be meaningful. Reading materials should be appropriate and should speak to adolescents' diverse interests and varying abilities.
- Student-chosen tasks must be supported with appropriate instructional support or scaffolding.[18]

B. Responsive Classroom Environments

- Caring, responsive classroom environments enable students to take ownership of literacy activities and can counteract negative emotions that lead to lack of motivation.

- Instruction should center around learners. Active, inquiry-based activities engage reluctant academic readers and writers. Inquiry-based writing connects writing practices with real-world experiences and tasks.
- Experiences with task-mastery enable increased self-efficacy, which leads to continued engagement.
- Demystifying academic literacy helps adolescents stay engaged.
- Using technology is one way to provide learner-centered, relevant activities. For example, many students who use computers to write show more engagement and motivation and produce longer and better papers.
- Sustained experiences with diverse texts in a variety of genres that offer multiple perspectives on life experiences can enhance motivation, particularly if texts include electronic and visual media.[19]

4. Value of Multicultural Perspectives

Monocultural approaches to teaching can cause or increase the achievement gap and adolescents' disengagement with literacy. Students should see value in their own cultures and the cultures of others in their classrooms. Students who do not find representations of their own cultures in texts are likely to lose interest in school-based literacies. Similarly, they should see their home languages as having value. Those whose home language is devalued in the classroom will usually find school less engaging.

Research says . . .

Multicultural literacy is seeing, thinking, reading, writing, listening, and discussing in ways that critically confront and bridge social, cultural, and personal differences. It goes beyond a "tourist" view of cultures and encourages engagement with cultural issues in all literature, in all classrooms, and in the world.[20]

A. Multicultural Literacy across All Classrooms

- Multicultural education does not by itself foster cultural inclusiveness because it can sometimes reinforce stereotypical perceptions that need to be addressed critically.
- Multicultural literacy is not just a way of reading "ethnic" texts or discussing issues of "diversity," but rather is a holistic way of *being* that fosters social responsibility and extends well beyond English/language arts classrooms.
- Teachers need to acknowledge that we all have cultural frameworks within which we operate, and everyone—teachers and students alike—needs to consider how these frameworks can be challenged or changed to benefit all peoples.[21]
- Teacher knowledge of social science, pedagogical, and subject-matter content knowledge about diversity will foster adolescents' learning.
- Successful literacy development among English language learners depends on and fosters collaborative multicultural relationships among researchers, teachers, parents, and students.
- Integration of technology will enhance multicultural literacy.

- Confronting issues of race and ethnicity within classrooms and in the larger community will enhance student learning and engagement.[22]

B. Goals of Multicultural Literacy

- Students will view knowledge from diverse ethnic and cultural perspectives, and use knowledge to guide action that will create a humane and just world.
- Teachers will help students understand the whiteness studies principle that white is a race so they can develop a critical perspective on racial thinking by people of all skin colors.
- Multicultural literacy will serve as a means to move between cultures and communities and develop transnational understandings and collaboration.
- Ideally, students will master basic literacies *and* become multiculturally literate citizens who foster a democratic multicultural society.[23]

Research-Based Recommendations for Effective Adolescent Literacy Instruction

For teachers . . .

Research on the practices of highly effective adolescent literacy teachers reveals a number of common qualities. Teachers who have received recognition for their classroom work, who are typically identified as outstanding by their peers and supervisors, and whose students consistently do well on high-stakes tests share a number of qualities. These qualities, in order of importance, include the following:

1. teaching with approaches that foster critical thinking, questioning, student decision-making, and independent learning;
2. addressing the diverse needs of adolescents whose literacy abilities vary considerably;
3. possessing personal characteristics such as caring about students, being creative and collaborative, and loving to read and write;
4. developing a solid knowledge about and commitment to literacy instruction;
5. using significant quality and quantity of literacy activities including hands-on, scaffolding, mini-lessons, discussions, group work, student choice, ample feedback, and multiple forms of expression;
6. participating in ongoing professional development;
7. developing quality relationships with students; and
8. managing the classroom effectively.[24]

For school programs . . .

Research on successful school programs for adolescent literacy reveals fifteen features that contribute to student achievement:

1. direct and explicit instruction;
2. effective instructional principles embedded in content;

3. motivation and self-directed learning;

4. text-based collaborative learning;

5. strategic tutoring;

6. diverse texts;

7. intensive writing;

8. technology;

9. ongoing formative assessment of students;

10. extended time for literacy;

11. long-term and continuous professional development, especially that provided by literacy coaches;

12. ongoing summative assessment of students and programs;

13. interdisciplinary teacher teams;

14. informed administrative and teacher leadership; and

15. comprehensive and coordinated literacy program.[25]

For policymakers . . .

A national survey produced action steps for policymakers interested in fostering adolescent literacy. These include:

1. align the high school curriculum with postsecondary expectations so that students are well prepared for college;

2. focus state standards on the essentials for college and work readiness;

3. shape high school courses to conform with state standards;

4. establish core course requirements for high school graduation;

5. emphasize higher-level reading skills across the high school curriculum;

6. make sure students attain the skills necessary for effective writing;

7. ensure that students learn science process and inquiry skills; and

8. monitor and share information about student progress.[26]

This report is produced by NCTE's James R. Squire Office of Policy Research, directed by Anne Ruggles Gere, with assistance from Laura Aull, Hannah Dickinson, Melinda McBee Orzulak, and Ebony Elizabeth Thomas, all students in the Joint PhD Program in English and Education at the University of Michigan.

Notes

1. ACT. (2006). *Aligning postsecondary expectations and high school practice: The gap defined: Policy implications of the ACT national curriculum survey results 2005–2006.* Iowa City, IA. Retrieved on July 3, 2007, from http://www.act.org/path/policy/pdf/NationalCurriculum Survey2006.pdf

Adolescent Literacy

Applebee, A., & Langer, J. (2006). *The state of writing instruction in America's schools: What existing data tell us*. Center on English Learning and Achievement. Retrieved on July 3, 2007, from http://cela.albany.edu

National Center for Education Statistics. (2002). *National Assessment of Educational Progress (NAEP). NAEP Writing–Average writing scale score results, grades 4, 8, and 12: 1998 and 2002*. Retrieved on July 3, 2007, from http://nces.ed.gov/nationsreportcard/writing/results2002/natscalescore.asp

National Center for Education Statistics. (2006). *National Assessment of Educational Progress (NAEP). Reading Results: Executive Summary for Grades 4 and 8*. Retrieved on July 3, 2007, from http://nces.ed.gov/nationsreportcard/reading/

2. Altwerger, B., Arya, P., Jin, L., Jordan, N. L., et al. (2004). When research and mandates collide: The challenges and dilemmas of teacher education in the era of NCLB. *English Education, 36*, 119–133.

National Center on Education and the Economy. (2007). *Tough choices or tough times: The report of the New Commission on the Skills of the American Workforce*. San Francisco, CA: Jossey-Bass.

3. Brandt, D. (2001). *Literacy in American lives*. New York: Cambridge University Press.

Gee, J. (2007). *Social linguistics and literacies: Ideology in discourses*. London: Taylor & Francis.

4. Franzak, J. K. (2006). *Zoom*. A review of the literature on marginalized adolescent readers, literacy theory, and policy implications. *Review of Educational Research, 76*, 2, 209–248.

5. Sturtevant, E., & Linek, W. (2003). The instructional beliefs and decisions of middle and secondary teachers who successfully blend literacy and content. *Reading Research & Instruction, 43*, 74–90.

6. Guzzetti, B., & Gamboa, M. (2004). 'Zines for social justice: Adolescent girls writing on their own. *Reading Research Quarterly, 39*, 408–437.

Langer, J. (2001). Beating the odds: Teaching middle and high school students to read and write well. *American Educational Research Journal, 38*, 4, 837–880.

Nielsen, L. (2006). Playing for real: Texts and the performance of identity. In D. Alvermann, K. Hinchman, D. Moore, S. Phelps, & D. Waff (Eds.), *Reconceptualizing the literacies in adolescents' lives* (2nd ed.) Mahwah, NJ: Lawrence Erlbaum, 5–28.

Sturtevant, E. & Linek, W. (2003).

7. Moje, E. B. (2002). Re-framing adolescent literacy research for new times: Studying youth as a resource. *Reading Research and Instruction, 41*, 211–228.

8. Boscolo, P., & Mason, L. (2001). Writing to learn, writing to transfer. In G. Jijlaarsdam, P. Tynjala, L. Mason, & K. Londa (Eds.), *Studies in writing: Vol 7. Writing as a learning tool: Integrating theory and practice*. Dordrecht, The Netherlands: Kluwer Academic Publishers, 83–104.

9. Lenters, K. (2006). Resistance, struggle, and the adolescent reader. *Journal of Adolescent and Adult Literacy, 50*(2), 136–142.

10. Moje, E. B., & Sutherland, L. M. (2003). The future of middle school literacy education. *English Education, 35*(2), 149–164.

Snow, C. E., & Biancarosa, G. (2003). *Adolescent literacy and the achievement: What do we know and where do we go from here?* New York: Carnegie Corporation. Retrieved June 23, 2007, from http://www.all4ed.org/resources/CarnegieAdolescentLiteracyReport.pdf

11. Bangert-Drowns, R. L., Hurley, M. M., & Wilkinson, B. (2004). The effects of school-based writing-to-learn interventions on academic achievement: A meta-analysis. *Review of Educational Research, 74*, 29–58.

Greenleaf, C. L., Schoenbach, R., Cziko, C., & Mueller, F. (2001). Apprenticing adolescent readers to academic literacy. *Harvard Education Review, 71*(1), 79–129.

12. Moje, E. B., Ciechanowski, K. M, Kramer, K., Ellis, L., Carrillo, R., & Collazo, T. (2004). Working toward third space in content area literacy: An examination of everyday funds of knowledge and discourse. *Reading Research Quarterly, 39*(1), 38–70.

13. Moje, E. B. (2007). Developing socially just subject-matter instruction: A review of the literature on disciplinary literacy. N. L. Parker (Ed.), *Review of research in education.* (pp. 1–44). Washington, DC: American Educational Research Association.

14. Kim, J. L. W., & Monique, L. (2004). Pleasure reading: Associations between young women's sexual attitudes and their reading of contemporary women's magazines. *Psychology of Women Quarterly, 28*(1), 48–58.

Kliewer, C., Biklen, D., & Kasa-Hendrickson, C. (2006). Who may be literate? Disability and resistance to the cultural denial of competence. *American Educational Research Journal, 43*(2), 163–192.

Moje, E. B., & Sutherland, L. M. (2003).

15. Moje, E. B. (2007).

Ross, C. S. (2001). Making choices: What readers say about choosing books for pleasure. In W. Katz (Ed.), *Reading, Books, and Librarians.* New York: Haworth Information Press.

16. Guthrie, J. T., Van Meter, P., McCann, A. D., Wigfield, A., Bennett, L., & Poundstone, C. C. (1996). Growth of literacy engagement: Changes in motivations and strategies during concept-oriented reading instruction. *Reading Research Quarterly, 31*, 306–332.

17. Guthrie, J. T. (2001). Contexts for engagement and motivation in reading. *Reading Online.* International Reading Association. Retrieved June 23, 2007, from http://www.readingonline.org/articles/handbook/guthrie/index.html

Guthrie, J. T., & Humenick, N. M. (2004). Motivating students to read: Evidence for classroom practices that increase reading motivation and achievement. In P. McCardle and V. Chhabra (Eds.), *The voice of evidence in reading research.* Baltimore, MD: Brookes, 329–54.

Adolescent Literacy

18. Biancarosa, G., & Snow, C. (2004). *Reading next: A vision for action and research in middle and high school literacy. Report to Carnegie Corporation of New York.* Washington, DC: Alliance for Excellent Education. Retrieved June 25, 2007, from http://www.all4ed.org/publications/ReadingNext/ReadingNext.pdf

Guthrie, J. T. (2001).

Oldfather, P. (1994). *When students do not feel motivated for literacy learning: How a responsive classroom culture helps.* College Park, MD: University of Maryland, National Reading Research Center. Retrieved June 25, 2007, from http://curry.edschool.virginia.edu/go/clic/nrrc/rspon_r8.html; NCREL (2005).

19. Goldberg, A., Russell, M., & Cook, A. (2003). The effects of computers on student writing: A meta-analysis of studies from 1992 to 2002. *Journal of Technology, Learning, and Assessment, 2,* 1–51.

Greenleaf et al. (2001).

Guthrie, J. T. (2001).

Kamil, M. (2003).

Ray, K. W. (2006). Exploring inquiry as a teaching stance in the writing workshop. *Language Arts, 83*(3), 238–248.

20. Hade, D. (1997). Reading multiculturally. In V. Harris (Ed.), *Using multiethnic literature in the K-8 classroom.* Norwood: Christopher-Gordon.

Cai, M. (1998). Multiple definitions of multicultural literature: Is the debate really just "ivory tower" bickering? *New Advocate, 11,* 4, 11–24.

Taxel, J. (1992). The politics of children's literature: Reflections on multiculturalism, political correctness, and Christopher Columbus. In V. Harris (Ed.), *Teaching multicultural literature in grades K-8.* Norwood: Christopher-Gordon.

21. Fang, Z., Fu, D., & Lamme, L. (1999). Rethinking the role of multicultural literature in literacy instruction: Problems, paradox, and possibilities. *New Advocate, 12*(3), 259–276.

Nieto, S. (2000). *Affirming diversity: The sociopolitical context of multicultural education.* New York: Longman.

Rochman, H. (1993). Beyond political correctness. In D. Fox & K. Short (Eds.), *Stories matter: The complexity of cultural authenticity in children's literature.* Urbana: NCTE.

Taxel, J. (1992).

22. Banks, J. A. (1991). Teaching multicultural literacy to teachers. *Teaching Education, 4,* 1, 135–144.

Feuerverger, G. (1994). A multicultural literacy intervention for minority language students. *Language and Education, 8,* 3, 123–146.

Diamond, B. J., & Moore, M. A. (1995). Multicultural literacy: Mirroring the reality of the classroom. New York: Longman.

Freedman, S. W. (1999). *Inside city schools: Investigating literacy in multicultural classrooms.* New York: Teachers College Press.

23. Banks, J. A. (2004). *Handbook of research on multicultural education*. San Francisco: Jossey-Bass.

Jay, G. S. (2005). Whiteness studies and the multicultural literature classroom. *MELUS, 30*(2), 99-121.

Luke, A., & Carpenter, M. (2003). Literacy education for a new ethics of global community. *Language Arts, 81*(1), 20.

24. Applebee, A., Langer, J., Nystrand, M., & Gamoran, A. (2003). Discussion-based approaches to developing understanding: Classroom instruction and student performance in middle and high school English. *American Educational Research Journal, 40*, 685–730.

Paris, S. R., & Block, C. C. (2007). The expertise of adolescent literacy teachers. *Journal of Adolescent & Adult Literacy, 50*, 7, 582–596.

25. Biancarosa, G., & Snow, C. E. (2004).

26. ACT, 2006.

This publication of the James R. Squire Office of Policy Research offers updates on research with implications for policy decisions that affect teaching and learning. Each issue addresses a different topic. Download this issue at http://www.ncte.org/library/NCTEFiles/Resources/Positions/chron0907ResearchBrief.pdf.

English Teacher or Reading Teacher? A Wake-Up Call

Last fall I entered a classroom to meet my new group of literature students. I've been greeting new students, grades 9 through college, every fall for more than three decades. But this group of students was different. The classroom was in a maximum security prison. The students were all convicted felons, many with life sentences, and most incarcerated before their twenty-first birthday. The course was an introduction to literature class and I began it, as I always do, with a reading autobiography.

"When did you begin to read?" I asked. "What did you love about reading? Were you a successful reader in school? What books do you remember most vividly?"

Perhaps not surprising, there was a flood of stories about unsuccessful reading experiences, low-track reading groups, and, eventually, a slow but certain movement away from school to the streets.

"I love reading now," said one student. "It actually is saving my life. But I hated it in school."

"I don't think I ever really learned to read well," said another, "and I sure didn't like the stuff we read. I had teachers who were cool enough, but they seemed to be teaching books, but not how to read them."

"If only reading had worked for me then," another student chimed in, "who knows what my path would have been?"

As I listened, I felt my face flush with guilt. I'm an English teacher and proud of it. I teach adolescents how to make meaning with literary texts. I also teach future teachers how to do the same. But I am not nor have I ever considered myself a *reading* teacher. Teaching young people to appreciate literature was my calling, I thought. Let others deal with decoding!

So what am I doing writing a book on teaching reading? Like many of you, I want to know more about how to help my students who either can't or won't read. And I need to learn how to tell the difference. If there is one thing my stint as a prison teacher has taught me, it's that the consequences of not providing critical literacy skills to *all* of my students are just too high.

English Teacher or Reading Teacher

There was a time when the reading teacher and the English teacher were clearly different people. Traditionally, English teachers have viewed themselves as literature teachers and have seen their task as building upon the foundations established by reading teachers. First we learn to read; then we read literature. This dichotomy entails a fundamental misunderstanding about what reading is: a distinction that lies somewhere between comprehension and analysis, or maybe even between knowledge and comprehension. Successful *reading*, we now know, crosses these cognitive boundaries, this false opposition between teaching reading and teaching literature.

For a variety of reasons, however, traceable perhaps to initial preservice training, teaching philosophy, state licensure requirements, and eventual teaching assignments, our field of language arts is often divided between those of us who consider ourselves to be primarily teachers of literature and those of us who consider ourselves to be teachers of reading. Yet, ideally, as a student experiences our English classes, aren't these two previously separated fields or perspectives really one and the same? Aren't teachers of literature and teachers of reading ultimately teachers of literacy? And isn't it time we come together to consider how to address the causes for concern in adolescent literacy, as outlined by *Adolescent Literacy: An NCTE Policy Research Brief*?

Over the last twenty or so years, the field of English education has undergone a shift. Research on the teaching of literature and research on the teaching of reading have converged in considering many of the same factors, from the cognitive processes involved in reading to the particular contextual factors that influence a student's reading to larger social cultural considerations that affect literacy learning. Contemporary scholars, such as Alverman et al.; Applebee; Beach and Myers; Graves and Graves; Langer; Wilhelm, etc., draw on the theoretical underpinnings of both reading research and research that focuses on response to literature to help teachers choose texts, establish learning environments, create lessons, and design methods of assessment that help ensure every student's reading success.

There also has been an explosion of research on the various factors that affect and inform students' literacy learning. For example, much recent literacy research has focused on the degree to which gender influences students' reading ability and interests (Pirie; Newkirk; Smith and Wilhelm, *Reading*), while others have explored the relationship of out-of-school contexts and literacies to school-based academic performance in reading and writing (Hull and Schultz; Morrell; Fisher).

What does all this mean for you as an English teacher? Clearly, you *are* teaching both literature and reading, but if you're like many English teachers, the increased emphasis on teaching reading may seem a bit outside of your professional identity. What I want to argue in this text is that the connection between being a literature teacher and being a teacher of reading may be closer than you think.

Recent public outcry about the state of adolescent literacy hits me right in my teacher heart. After all, I have always thought that my work as an English teacher was, in the final analysis, designed to promote adolescent literacy. I assumed that the domain of explicit reading instruction was different from mine, but the conversation about adolescent literacy has forced me to reconsider my relationship to the teaching of reading. I have come to the conclusion that all teachers of literature are essentially teachers of reading.

Consider this definition offered by Frank Smith:

> My preferred description (of reading) in a general sense is: making sense of things. When you read someone's face, you're trying to make sense of what might be going on between the eyes. When you read the cloud formations in the evening, you're trying to make sense of what the weather might be like tomorrow. And when you read a printed page, you're trying to make sense of what is written on it. When you read a story, you try to interpret what it is about, to make sense of the story. You try to interpret what the characters are up to, or what was in the author's mind. You interpret in order to make sense of things. Interpretation is the fundamental way of life for all of us, from birth to final breath. We're always trying to figure out what is going on. (5)

Finally it dawned on me, what Dickie Self calls a "duh-piphany." Reading *is* interpreting; interpreting *is* reading. That means literature teachers are reading teachers, and in this age of exploding literacies it has never been more important to recognize that.

Shifting Literacy Demands

Tweeting, Facebooking, MySpacing, and text messaging—it seems that no matter where we look, adolescents are engaged in literate acts. Never have decoding and receiving messages been so widespread, and never have reading and producing texts been more important to adolescents. Young people today may seem, at first glance, to be multiliterate in many contexts, and they are. At the same time, though, there are signs that point to a crisis in literacy among adolescents. While new media provide abundant channels for adolescent communication and self-expression, the traditional literacies abide, looming like gates in front of those who do not know them. Welcome to the twenty-first century, where images of adolescent literacy have never been more promising nor more challenging.

And so the battle lines form, between the traditions that define communicative competence in the larger world and the fascinating inventions of the self and its surroundings that spring from the machinery of youth culture. Virtual social networks exist on both sides of this line. Technology is neither friend nor enemy. What it is, though, is beyond the control of teachers.

And this whole world is far too new to allow us to predict its future. Perhaps like the preadolescent linguistic forms of neighborhood games, with their own vocabularies and communicative rituals (remember "duck-duck-goose" and "ally-ally-in-come-free"?), the adolescent forms of texting will prove to be only a linguistic tunnel out of which young people eventually emerge. Perhaps, on the other hand, the communicative rituals now privileged by school, government, and commerce will be the ones left behind as young people emerge into adulthood and claim these new literacies as the new status quo.

And so our challenge takes its shape. We don't know what the future of literacy looks like, and yet we are charged with leading our students into it. The challenge is magnified by their skepticism about our practices. Our practices, many teens seem to claim, are narrow in their social scope, confined largely to the middle class and those who aspire upward from there. Our practices are limited in their creativity, perhaps because young people define *creativity* in language differently from, say, Noam Chomsky. While *we* understand that nearly every sentence of academic prose in English is perhaps unique in the history of the language, many young people see only a language that belongs to us and not to them. They imagine us attempting to sell it to them, and at a high cost. We shouldn't be surprised that many are not buying it.

The Literacy Crisis

All of these factors, together with the increased prominence of standardized tests in the educational landscape, have helped fuel public concern about a literacy crisis. Almost annually, federal reports such as *Reading at Risk: A Survey of Literary Reading in America* (NEA, 2004), *Reading Next: A Vision for Action and Research in Middle and High School Literacy* (Carnegie, 2004), *The Nation's Report Card: Reading* (NCE, 2007), and the most recent *To Read or Not to Read: A Question of National Consequence* (NEA, 2007) point to the need for increased attention to how we teach students to read. Report after report documents the changing demands of literacy in a digital age and our collective fear that our schools are not meeting the basic literacy needs of our adolescents. Additionally, more pressure has been placed on all classroom teachers because of mandated reporting of academic progress in reading (as well as other subjects) by the No Child Left Behind Act.

And many students who can read don't seem to want to after they leave our classrooms. Kathleen Yancey quotes a study of students' out-of-school activities that found that students participate in "78 minutes of reading compared to 12 hours of watching television" (2). A publication entitled *Popular Culture and the American Child* notes that more than 32 percent of teenagers claim that they never read, while only 18 percent claim to read often. Those who do encounter texts often do so in the context of new literacies from video games to instant messages. In fact, as Pirie and Gee (*What Video Games*) have argued, the role of the literature teacher may indeed be to help young people navigate those new literacies.

Adolescent Literacy: An NCTE Policy Research Brief, the starting point for this book, also cites studies in literacy achievement in an effort to help shape policy that informs literacy instruction. First, and perhaps most important in terms of the impetus for this volume, the brief offers a well-reasoned alarm for literacy teachers from all grades, citing a persistent gap in achievement between white students and students of color, and offering national assessment findings that show a lack of progress in reading and writing proficiency for all students over the past decade. The brief warns us that this lack of literacy proficiency may already have contributed to the increasingly smaller share that young U.S. workers hold in the global workforce. In other words, we have serious reason to worry about the welfare and future of adolescents, both in and out of school.

The brief provides research-based summaries of four important areas related to our understanding of adolescent literacy:

1. *Shifting literacy demands*, as students shift to secondary schools that emphasize content-based classrooms and, of course, the proliferation of high-stakes tests;

2. *Multiple and social literacies*, which refer to the various discourse communities, in and out of school, to which our students belong;

3. *The importance of motivation*, which reminds us that it is the level of motivation

as much as the level of literacy skill that will determine whether a student engages in literacy learning; and

4. *The value of multicultural perspectives*, which reminds us that all students need to see their own cultures reflected in the texts we read and their home language valued in the classroom.

These factors are key considerations as we literature teachers try to integrate research-based principles into our practice, a goal that undergirds this and all volumes in the Principles in Practice imprint.

Reports such as *Adolescent Literacy: An NCTE Policy Research Brief* and the National Endowment for the Arts research report *To Read or Not to Read* remind us that while "new literacies" may be on the upswing, performance on traditional literacy measures is declining at alarming and consistent rates. Fewer students are choosing to read and fewer students are reading at grade level. In addition, despite what some might characterize as an unfortunate overemphasis on testing and teaching to the test, the achievement gap, the gap between different segments of America's student population, is growing ever wider. In fact, some educational observers opine that the emphasis on standards and tests has only served to widen both the achievement gap and the "opportunity" gap, as students who attend under-resourced schools continue to fall behind their more privileged peers on standardized measures of achievement. Regardless of one's political or philosophical persuasion, it is painfully clear that No Child Left Behind has indeed left many children and adolescents, as well as their teachers, in the throes of a significant literacy crisis.

As English teachers, we must heed the call of this new crisis, without defensiveness or apology. As English or language or communication arts teachers, we are at the front line of fostering adolescent literacy. We may feel as if we have been doing our job to the best of our abilities and that there is a constellation of factors beyond our control that have contributed to this literacy crisis. That is undoubtedly true. And still, we need to face the challenging terrain of contemporary adolescent literacy and remap our pedagogical strategies. For English teachers, when it comes to what is arguably the core component of adolescent literacy, reading, many of us have not felt ready to heed the call.

The Changing Literature Classroom

Being a teacher of literature now means much more than finding innovative ways to help our students experience literary texts. Being an English teacher now means—and at some pragmatic level probably always has meant—helping students make meaning as they read, a goal shared by teachers of literature and teachers of reading. We all have to answer the same questions as we enter our classrooms today: "What does it mean to read well? What do my students need to do to read a text successfully?" There was a time when reading teachers and literature teachers may have answered these questions differently. As Pat Monahan writes,

> If administrators had asked me ten years ago if I was teaching reading, I would have proudly answered, "Yes," for I heard them asking me if I was doing anything to help students read a novel *more fully* or *more completely*. In other words, do I help them to understand the book or get more out of it? Of course I do, and such an interpretation of reading instruction led me to literary criticism in an effort to ensure that students understood "everything" about a book. In fact, I felt guilty if I left anything out.
>
> Today, however, I hear the question differently. Now I hear administrators asking me if my teaching of the book supports students' development as critical readers, and, if so, am I aware of how my teaching influences their learning to read? Am I deliberately teaching reading behaviors? I also hear them asking me if I do anything to help students become independent readers, actively involved in books and less reliant on teachers. (98)

Today we can agree that our students all need to accomplish the same goals as they read: an accurate decoding, full comprehension, visualization, analysis of message, recognition of assumptions, and construction of meaning. The complexity and types of texts our students read may change in different settings, but the challenges of reading are the same for every student.

In addition to the changes of emphasis in our field, the composition of our classrooms also has changed over the last two decades. Most English classrooms are larger and more diverse than they were even five years ago. In many cases, classrooms are more under-resourced, as the funding for public schools has shrunk, and money for new materials has become increasingly difficult to come by. More schools have higher populations of high-poverty students. The literacy experiences and backgrounds of our students vary dramatically. Our classrooms are filled with students whose cultural backgrounds and stances toward mainstream learning practices may vary widely (Tatum, *Teaching*; Ogbu; Mahiri). They are increasingly filled with students for whom English is not their first language. They are also filled with students who, while demonstrating proficiency in digital forms of literacy, sometimes have difficulty transferring that proficiency to traditional literacy acts such as reading literary texts or writing essays (Gee, *What Video Games*; Beers).

Our increased ability to assess and monitor students' progress in reading has helped us realize what has probably been true for decades: that our literature classrooms are filled with a number of students who are not reading at grade level, and that while students may be able to decode the texts we assign, many students may not derive sufficient meaning or pleasure from texts simply because they are not adequately and specifically prepared to read them. Today, we realize that successful reading also entails recognition of context, attitude, ambiguity, and the possibility of multiple meanings. Success at these tasks translates to enjoyment of reading; failure leads to frustration—and, very likely, the lack of motivation that we see as one of the hallmarks of adolescent literacy.

For these reasons, today's English teachers likely feel tugged in seemingly opposite directions. We feel a sense of urgency to do everything in our power to foster productive literacy practices among our students, to make certain that they are successful readers and academic writers. On the other hand, we don't want to lose the texture, richness, and autonomy of our literature classrooms. We worry this is what will happen if our pedagogy is held hostage to standardized tests. We often still labor under the mistaken notion that improving kids' reading is accomplished only through explicit reading instruction in centralized and standardized reading programs.

While there is clearly some justification for a sense of urgency with regard to adolescent literacy, English teachers need not succumb to a mistaken conclusion that increased attention to improving students' reading strategies would shift the instructional focus from literature to "drill and skills." This book explores the ways in which reading instruction can and should be embedded within our literature instruction.

Issues in Adolescent Reading

In keeping with the aims of this imprint series, this book describes some of the issues surrounding adolescent reading and how those issues in particular connect to those of us who are literature teachers. It reviews current literature around the topic and then offers practical strategies for teachers.

In Chapter 2, I summarize the most recent and promising developments in reading research over the last decade or so. In keeping with the research-based principles approach of these volumes in the Principles in Practice imprint, my goal in this chapter is to share with busy teachers what research has helped us learn about the state of adolescent literacy and reading instruction, citing and unpacking a host of reports that decry the current effectiveness of literacy instruction. I then consider recent research on both cognitive and sociocultural contexts of literacy learning, focusing on the implications of these approaches for the language arts classroom. Finally, I suggest the most important principles gleaned from recent research on reading for the literature teacher.

In Chapter 3, I explore the expanding definition of the concept of "text," a concept that I believe is at the heart of English teaching. For many literature teachers, *text* too often refers solely to canonical literature. In this chapter, I ask what it might mean if we expand that term in ways that will benefit adolescent readers. What, for example, are the demands various texts place on readers—from text messaging, an alternative literacy that many teachers fear will interfere with students' mastery of traditional literacy practices, to classic novels. In this chapter, I also explore some classroom practices that assist students in seeing a range of literacies in their own experiences and the diversity of forms that literacy can take. Throughout the chapter, my goal is to help literature teachers rethink what we mean by a "text" and, in turn, what we mean by reading. If we are successful in expanding our notions of successful and engaged literacy practices, we will be better able to reach students who appear to be on the margins of our classroom but who really are engaged in literate acts.

Building on some of the concepts introduced in Chapter 1, Chapter 4 explores the relationship between teaching reading and teaching literature. It attempts to illustrate a variety of definitions for *reading* so that teachers can better imagine the relationship between mainstream literature instruction and the teaching of reading. It includes some specific examples of how a literature lesson can be reframed to more explicitly include reading strategies.

After a detailed classroom vignette, Chapter 5 distills the research-based principles of reading instruction to help all language arts teachers be able to help struggling readers improve. Building on what we've learned about recent research on reading, in Chapter 5 I offer some specific ways in which reading strategies can be integrated into whole-class literature instruction.

Chapter 6 explores one area of reading that has been the focus of much literacy research: that of gender and its impact on reading practices (Smith and Wilhelm, *Reading*; Smith, *Talking*; Mahar). Most simply put, girls often identify themselves as avid readers; boys frequently do not. Preferences for reading material also appear gendered, with boys articulating preferences for action books, science fiction, or plot-driven stories, whereas girls tend to prefer character-driven stories. These gendered predispositions toward reading affect both male and female roles in the literature classroom as well as their reading habits. Chapter 6 provides research-based strategies for encouraging all of our students to become better readers.

In Chapter 7, I begin with an acknowledgment of the degree to which standardized assessment drives the public's perception of what we think we know about how students are reading. Classroom teachers, on the other hand, need an array of assessment tools to offer alternatives to the single-point measure of standardized tests. The chapter discusses the importance of offering students formative assessment throughout their literature instruction. Finally, the chapter provides many examples of formative assessment that can be easily incorporated into a teacher's regular literature curriculum.

Chapter 8 offers suggestions for extending the community of readers of our classroom into the community at large. To be inclined to read into adulthood, adolescents need to see reading as an act that adults voluntarily engage in. Finally, the chapter considers the ways in which we can encourage adolescents, who too often read because we require them do so, to become adults who read out of their own desire.

The final chapter addresses a variety of issues related to the literacy crisis with a set of new "first principles" for the teaching of literature. These principles are motivated by an admonition to resist the one-size-fits-all solutions that national literacy standards and standardized testing too frequently suggest. Chapter 9 also includes some pragmatic suggestions for designing literature instruction to provide for the continuous development of reading skills such that all teachers of language arts will foster adolescent literacy as teachers of reading.

This, then, is the blueprint for our exploration into the reframing of our notion of what it means to be a literature teacher in the era of a crisis in adolescent literacy. Yes, as *Adolescent Literacy: An NCTE Policy Research Brief* reminds us, there is some urgency to this crisis, though in truth the urgency has always been there. We just didn't always see it. I want to make sure that every literature teacher is also a reading teacher, a teacher of literacy. As my incarcerated students so poignantly reminded me, we cannot afford to do less.

Chapter Two

What We Know about Adolescent Reading and What Literature Teachers Need to Know

In Chapter 1, I argued that there is a pedagogical and ideological divide between those who think of themselves as reading teachers and those who consider themselves to be literature teachers, and that divide is not working for our students. Somehow, then, we need to bridge the gap that divides us philosophically and pedagogically. We need to articulate how research-based principles of literature instruction can be in concert with research-based principles of reading instruction. That means, among other things, that we have to discover or rediscover what researchers and classroom teachers have come to know about adolescent reading and how that knowledge can reshape or reframe not only our literature instruction but also how we think about what it means to teach literature to adolescents.

To ground our literacy teaching practice in research-based principles, we need to first examine what those principles are. This can seem overwhelming, since the world and the word as we know them both in and out of the class-room are rapidly changing. In the twenty-first century, in an increasingly technological and globalized world, the definition of what literacy means for adolescents is changing as well. We have experienced an information explosion, surrounded by instant, electronic texts on our cell phones, our mp3 players, our computers, our televisions, even our cars.

As our concept of literacy changes, so too must our understanding of reading, the foundational literacy skill. The last few decades have seen a parallel explosion of what we know about adolescent literacy in general and about reading in particular. Researchers have learned a great deal about the cognitive processes that undergird reading, that is, mental activities that help readers make meaning of texts as they read. Researchers from a variety of fields, including psychology, linguistics, and literacy, have discovered ways in which learning to read shares significant similarities with the acquisition and development of other cognitive skills related to language acquisition, such as speech and writing.

In addition to the specific nature of the cognitive dimension of reading, researchers have broadened their analytic lens to explore what is often called the sociocultural dimension of reading, that is, the ways in which the process of making meaning through texts is situated within a variety of nontextual factors, including the cultural background and social context of the learner as well as the characteristics of the contexts, both school and nonschool, in which the learning takes place. So, what in all that research is vital for high school English teachers—especially those who think of themselves primarily as literature teachers—to know about reading? In this chapter, as I continue to articulate principles in the context of practice, I briefly discuss some of the major developments in current research about adolescent reading and how those principles can inform our classroom practice.

Clearly, the landscape of reading research has changed drastically in the last three decades. Both the object of study and the methods of studying it have undergone major transformations. Reading research has moved from a microscopic focus on letters and syllables to a more macroscopic notion that reading is a complex process situated within dynamic social, psychological, and cultural contexts.

In addition to this changing conception of reading, the methodology of reading research has changed (Christenbury, Bomer, and Smagorinsky). Research on reading has become less prescriptive and positivistic—some might argue less *scientific*—in nature. In addition to quantitative methods, research on reading now incorporates qualitative methods characterized by the thick, narrative approach of ethnography to capture the ecology of literacy practices in situated contexts (O'Brien et al.). Reading research now tries to tell stories of readers reading and of teachers teaching reading. It draws not only on the behavioral and cognitive traditions of the past but also on cultural studies, sociocultural theory, and discourse analysis.

It's important to note that there is a significant ideological and method-ological rift between the paradigm of more ethnographic or narrative qualitative research and the quantitative approaches that appear to be favored by groups such as the National Reading Panel, which have contributed years of contestations and controversy as the reading wars, both fairly and unfairly reported, have dragged on (Shanahan). This rift has led to profound political and pedagogical consequences, especially in the shadow of federal legislation such as No Child Left Behind and the more recent Race to the Top legislation. The urgent need to empirically dem-onstrate improved student scores in reading proficiency has led to a privileging of a certain kind of quantitative research, which, in turn, trickles down into a reductive understanding of literacy and a tendency to focus on drill and skill. As some whole language advocates would put it:

> In findings decried by whole language advocates, who claimed much of the research on their approach was excluded unfairly, the panel recommended explicit instruction in five areas: phonemic awareness, referring to a grasp of the sounds that make up words; phonics; vocabulary; fluency; and comprehension. These became the "proven" methods rolled into the No Child Left Behind Act and Reading First, and they are the mainstays of most reading programs today. (Smydo 2)

These ideological wars may be beyond the immediate concern of most classroom teachers, but research on adolescent literacy has clearly been influenced by these rifts. Still, despite the contestations of methodology and scope, the past two decades have seen a wealth of literacy research on reading that is particularly helpful to the literature teacher. Given the enormous scope of reading research, it would be impossible to do it justice in this slim volume. Therefore, I want to focus on the developments that seem to hold the greatest promise and applicability for you as a classroom teacher of literature. These developments include understand-ing reading as a complex cognitive task, introducing students to the cognitive strategies embedded in reading as a kind of tool kit, integrating reading apprentice-ships into the academic curriculum, and recognizing the sociocultural dimensions of reading practices. All of these research perspectives have direct relevance to your secondary classroom.

Reading as a Complex Cognitive Task

Reading researchers have increasingly emphasized the notion that reading is a complex task consisting of a variety of cognitive strategies. These cognitive strate-gies include but are not limited to the following:

Cognitive Strategies in Reading

- Tapping prior knowledge
- Visualizing
- Summarizing
- Making connections
- Forming interpretations
- Monitoring
- Clarifying
- Revising meaning
- Evaluating

What researchers have discovered is that expert readers are able to make these reading strategies explicit or visible, whereas less able readers may not really be aware of what they are doing. In other words, expert readers have a kind of *metacognitive* understanding of how reading works and what they are doing when they read, whereas novice readers do not. Research on reading has focused on how those cognitive strategies can be made visible to less able readers so that they might be able to integrate those strategies into their reading. This line of research also has delineated particular approaches to reading instruction that make these strategies visible so that novice or less able readers can learn and then apply the strategies that eventually have become second nature to good readers.

Cognitive Strategies as a Tool Kit

Research that explicates the cognitive strategies that undergird reading has influenced the principles of reading instruction in at least two important ways. First is the notion of the mental tool kit. Borrowing liberally from the work of Russian psychologist Lev Vygotsky, several researcher–practitioners have introduced this idea of a *tool kit* of cognitive strategies that can be explicitly taught to novice readers, who then are able to draw on them as they read. As Carol Booth Olson points out in her extremely useful *The Reading/Writing Connection*, teachers can help students understand the cognitive strategies that are necessary for successful reading by thinking of them as specific tools that can be chosen knowingly by the reader, just as one reaches for a hammer to pound in a nail or a screwdriver to pull out a screw. For example, Olson suggests offering students a graphic of an actual tool kit that includes a variety of strategies, such as making predictions, asking questions, and visualizing. Such graphics help students understand the various strategies for creating meaning as they read. She advises teachers to explain it to students in the following way:

> So when you think of yourself as a reader or writer, think of yourself as a crafts-man, but instead of reaching into a mental tool kit for a hammer or a screwdriver to construct tangible objects, you're reaching into your mental tool kit for cognitive strategies like visualizing or making predictions to construct meaning from or with words. (21–22)

Integrating Reading Apprenticeships into the Literature Classroom

Another cognitively based approach that has been very helpful to secondary class-room teachers is the concept of reading apprenticeships. While several models of reading apprenticeships have been developed, Ruth Schoenbach and her colleagues at WestEd have presented a particularly useful model. Based on extensive research with secondary students, these literacy researchers have expanded the notion of what's known as a cognitive apprenticeship into a reading apprenticeship. Based on the work of researchers working within the social-cognitive tradition, Schoenbach and colleagues define a cognitive apprenticeship in this way: "The mental activi-ties characteristic of certain kinds of cognitive tasks such as computation, written composition, interpreting texts, and the like are internalized and appropriated by learners through social supports of various kinds" (21). In other words, learners learn by being introduced to a task, having that task modeled, and then trying it on their own with the support and the guidance of others. It's not unlike learning to ride a bicycle, with training wheels *and* a guiding hand behind the rider's back until she can take off on her own.

The reading apprenticeship framework builds on this model of cognitive ap-prenticeships as it integrates four key dimensions of classroom life—social, per-sonal, cognitive, and knowledge building—into an approach to reading instruction that focuses on academic literacy and metacognition. Teachers can make a reading apprenticeship an integral part of their curriculum through the incorporation of such techniques as reciprocal teaching, think-aloud protocols, partnered reading, whole-class discussion, and small-group discussion, as well as through the explicit teaching of strategies such as questioning, summarizing, predicting, and clarify-ing. The advantage of this model is that it can be easily integrated into mainstream secondary classrooms. In fact, the purpose of this approach is to teach students to think of reading as a central component of their academic literacy, whatever the discipline.

The proponents of this program describe, for example, how to embed reading apprenticeships into subject-area classrooms, such as science teachers incorporating metacognitive strategies of summarizing and clarifying to help their students understand complicated science texts or social studies teachers using think-alouds, in which a student comments on his own reading and identifies areas of confusion as well as questions he'd like to ask as he reads a social studies text. Schoenbach and her colleagues argue that every academic classroom should offer explicit instruction in reading strategies through these reading apprenticeships. If a math or social studies classroom can host reading apprenticeships, surely a literature classroom can do the same.

Jeffrey Wilhelm approaches this notion of reading apprenticeships from a slightly different perspective. Like Schoenbach and her colleagues, Wilhelm acknowledges the centrality of Vygotsky's work in which views children's cognitive development as being socially mediated; in other words, how we learn is dependent not just on our internal mental processes but on the social and cultural conditions in which those processes take place. In books such as *Improving Comprehension with Think-Aloud Strategies* and *Action Strategies for Deepening Comprehension*, Wilhelm and his colleagues argue that reading should be approached not as a skill but as a form of cognitive inquiry; that is, they stress the importance of explicitly teaching reading through strategies such as cognitive structuring, modeling, questioning, explaining/instructing, feeding back/naming, and contingency management. All of these strategies are designed to help students engage actively in their reading processes as intellectual inquiry. An important component of Wilhelm's argument is that these habits of inquiry will lead to lifelong literacy. Like the reading apprenticeship model, Wilhelm's approach stresses habits of mind and enduring stances toward learning rather than a discrete set of skills that often seem decontextualized. Wilhelm believes that teachers need to explicitly model what good readers do by combining very explicit instruction with explicit teaching of strategies such as visualizing, inferring, predicting, summarizing, self-monitoring, and questioning. Wilhelm believes that by using a think-aloud approach in which both teachers and students articulate their process of making meaning as they read, novice readers will be able to adopt the skills and strategies of expert readers, again an important thread in recent research on reading, and one that has particular resonance for the secondary literature teacher. After all, isn't our goal to help our literature students become able and expert readers?

What Olson's, Wilhelm's, and Schoenbach's work points to is the importance of scaffolding. While primary school teachers may not as easily question the need to explicitly model and scaffold reading processes, teachers of adolescents all too often assume that their students already possess the knowledge to be successful readers. Yet, as discussed, that is not always the case. Therefore, teachers need to be explicit about incorporating opportunities for modeling and scaffolding the complex processes of reading into their secondary classrooms, especially as reading becomes a part of each subject area with different demands, expectations, and approaches.

Schoenbach and her colleagues remind those of us who teach literature that our conception of reading may indeed be too narrow, which prevents us from addressing reading explicitly within our literature classrooms. They emphasize that the concept of reading that amounts to mastery of the skill of decoding is a "narrow, incomplete, and unproductive view of learning to read" and assert that "over two decades of research has shown that reading is a complex cognitive and social practice" (7). Here are the principles they have gleaned:

Research-Based Principles of Reading

- Reading is not just a basic skill.
- Reading is a complex process.
- Reading is problem solving.
- Fluent reading is not the same as decoding.
- Reading is situationally bounded.
- Proficient readers share some key characteristics.

It's Never Too Late

Another important thread that runs through the work of these researchers is the belief that it is never too late for adolescent readers to gain the skills they need to learn to read academic texts. Given the dire tone of much discourse about adolescent literacy both in the popular media and within academic communities, this is an assertion to keep in mind. Rather than despair over poor reading skills and the generally alarming state of adolescent literacy, we might be more successful if we consider our secondary English classrooms as a second chance for those adolescents lacking in literacy skills. As Schoenbach and her colleagues write, "the assumption that children who have not become good readers in the early grades will never catch up is both incorrect and destructive. Further, the companion assumption that children who learn to read well in those early years have no need of further reading instruction is also misguided" (6).

Recognizing the Sociocultural Dimensions of Reading Practices

Another way in which our understanding of reading has changed is through the frame of sociocultural research on literacy. Early reading research was very atomistic in nature, focused on particular aspects of reading as a discrete skill. To be sure, this focus is understandable, as early inquiry into reading focused on understanding the component parts that constitute the reading process and how those components might best be taught. Yet critical elements that undergird student performance in literacy tasks were not addressed by this research, factors including family literacy patterns and opportunities, community and individual identity, and membership in groups that traditionally had been marginalized or disenfranchised in school and society. In other words, because students' cultures and backgrounds are so different, we can't turn to one-size-fits-all reading instruction for them.

Recently, scholars such as Gee; Fairclough; Lewis, Enciso, and Moje; Compton-Lilly; Moll and Greenberg; Street; and others have brought to the forefront the ways in which these sociocultural factors impact student learning. While there are nearly as many approaches to sociocultural research on literacy as there are researchers, they generally share some of the following premises. First, sociocultural scholars believe that neither cognitive nor behavioral perspectives provide adequate explanations of such a complex phenomenon as learning. Second, as Lewis and colleagues point out, "Sociocultural theory has allowed us to explore the intersection of social, historical, mental, physical, and, more recently, political aspects of people's sense-making, interactions, and learning around texts" (2). In other words, sociocultural theorists think of learning as a mosaic comprising many individual tiles, which together help form a picture of how an individual learner approaches learning.

Sociocultural research also tells us what every middle and high school English teacher already knows: adolescents learn by talking and listening, especially to each other. Sociocultural theorists, then, consider literacy learning to be essentially a "social practice." Sociocultural theory as well considers a wide range of what Lewis and her colleagues call "mediating factors" that affect literacy learning and practice, factors such as the degree to which certain groups of literacy learners have been traditionally disenfranchised or marginalized in schools and society.

The fruits of this research, while perhaps messier and more inherently political than previous schools of literacy research, have proven to be particularly useful and robust to classroom teachers as they consider how best to structure literacy learning with their increasingly diverse group of learners. This research is particularly relevant to those of us who teach literature since the content of our literature curriculum, unlike mathematics or science, is neither fixed nor usually wholly predetermined. As our classrooms become increasingly diverse and as we continue to learn more about the importance of acknowledging the interplay between culture, literacy, and learning (Lee), the literature classroom is the ideal setting in which approaches to literacy can reflect what we have learned from this research. As Carol Jago reminds us, literary texts are both windows and mirrors, in which we can acknowledge the complexity, commonality, and difference of the social worlds in which we all reside. Situating the act of reading within those social worlds is an important implication of sociocultural research.

The Gap between Research and Practice

One persistent theme in research on reading is that, despite the advances in our understanding of what constitutes reading, we have not made the accompanying strides in improving adolescent literacy. For example, in an NCEE report, *Improving Adolescent Literacy: Effective Classroom and Intervention Practices*, the authors note that "reading instruction as a formal part of the curriculum typically decreases as students move beyond upper elementary grades" (4). In other words, even though data from a variety of national assessments demonstrate that more than a quarter of secondary students do not have "sufficient reading ability to understand and learn from text at their own reading level" (4), many content-area teachers, including English language arts teachers, still feel unprepared to integrate reading instruction into their secondary classrooms.

Part of the problem may be that, given the expansion of new literacies, even our definitions of reading proficiency may be antiquated and limiting. What we have come to believe about the nature of reading as a cognitive and academic skill—what it means to attain reading proficiency—has changed drastically as we confront new literacies. For example, O'Brien et al. (2009) argue that we must first expand our definitions of what it is that adolescents popularly read, as the texts they encounter expand to include Internet texts and more popular forms of texts such as manga. One example of how this awareness has reached the mainstream literature classroom is the growing use of graphic novels, such as *Persepolis*, into the high school canon of required and recommended texts. Some adolescents, especially those who may be labeled "reluctant readers" in traditional academic settings, may actually demonstrate proficiency in what's considered nonmainstream forms of literacy. In other words, they are not nonreaders; they are just not reading the texts that we assign in our English classrooms. If teachers can integrate some of these nontraditional texts into our literature instruction, we might be able to engage those reluctant learners. We'll further explore the implications of this as we consider strategies for working with "reluctant readers" in Chapter 5.

In addition to the kinds of texts adolescents are reading, the contexts in which they read those texts also have implications for proficiency. O'Brien et al. frame this as "situated practice." For example, a student reading a text for a book club will

The following are some ways in which sociocultural research has helped teachers reframe their classrooms.

Sociocultural Research in the Classroom

1. Teachers have incorporated their knowledge of student backgrounds into their curricular choices, widening the canon of commonly taught texts to include more diverse voices, including more works by writers of color as well as immigrant literature. In the Twin Cities of Minneapolis and St. Paul, for example, a metropolitan area with a large Hmong population, some teachers are developing curriculum around the first published memoir by Hmong American author Kao Kalia Yang, *The Late Homecomer*.

2. Teachers also have reconsidered their pedagogical practices in light of community norms and traditions by, for example, varying opportunities for both oral and written participation in class, honoring cultural tradition of expression through means other than traditional academic papers, and by carefully considering the social composition of the class when creating small groups in order to ensure feelings of comfort, safety, and belonging to all students.

3. Teachers also have become more aware of their own location with regard to positions of race, class, and privilege, and they have considered how those locations may inform student learning. For example, techniques such as sharing family stories or backgrounds—a favorite strategy for many English teachers, especially as a first step toward discussing particular pieces of literature—may not feel either comfortable or appropriate to certain students (Hynds and Appleman). With the help of writers such as Julie Landsman (*A White Teacher Talks about Race*), Gail Thompson (*Through Ebony Eyes*), Carol Lee (*Culture, Learning, and Literacy*), and Alfred Tatum, (*Reading for Their Life: (Re) Building the Textual Lineages of African American Adolescent Males*), teachers can honor the backgrounds of their students as they create their literature instruction.

4. Teachers have become increasingly mindful of the school–home connection, especially when thinking about early literacy experiences, communicating student progress, and offering enrichment opportunities for entire families. Many schools, for example, print their informational pamphlets and signs in several languages to include family members who may not be native English speakers. Teachers can also invite elders and other family members to visit their classrooms as community experts, thus honoring those traditions and, at the same time, integrating students' cultural funds of knowledge (Moll and Greenberg), that is, the valuable cultural information they bring to school, into their academic experience.

5. Teachers can design assignments that honor, rather than stigmatize, students' home languages. For example, one teacher I know who works with second language learners in rural Minnesota makes certain there are at least two Spanish speakers in each small group she constructs to ensure that no student feels linguistically stranded. In addition, she has added to her curriculum texts with Spanish words, poems that she presents in full translation, and diverse writers such as Gary Soto and Sandra Cisneros. Other teachers use cultural modeling to incorporate features of African American Vernacular English into their teaching.

6. Teachers can create opportunities for students to explore their cultural identity within the context of the language arts classroom. This kind of exploration can take many forms. For example, students can be encouraged to write cultural autobiographies in response to texts like *The House on Mango Street*, *Black Boy*, or *The Absolutely True Diary of a Part-Time Indian*.

read it very differently from how she might read it when it is assigned in a class. Additionally, students encounter a variety of texts and genres naturally throughout the day, texts that they access readily through their use of familiar technologies. This evolving nature of the interaction between adolescents and texts requires us to reconsider our definitions of both reading and reading proficiency. In other words, if students are exhibiting reading skills in textual encounters outside of school, we might need to think about how to incorporate the acknowledgment and development of those literacy skills within school. It is also important to acknowledge that different reading situations—reading a textbook in school, a billboard in a car, a magazine, or an email message—all require different skills.

In summary, what we have come to know about adolescent reading after two decades of reading research is this:

- Reading is a complex cognitive task with component parts.
- Approaching reading merely as an act of decoding leads to inadequate instruction.
- Like all literate acts, such as learning to speak and to write, reading is a socially mediated activity.
- Students benefit from explicit metacognitive instruction.
- Reading instruction can and should be embedded into all academic subject areas.
- Decontextualized reading instruction is not as effective as instruction that is embedded in authentic learning contexts.
- Teachers need to take into account the implications of the sociocultural contexts of reading as they consider instruction.
- It is never too late to engage adolescents successfully in reading.
- Adolescents' interest in new media and new literacies can be successfully translated into more academic literacies.

Given what we know about adolescents and reading, how can we translate what we know into effective classroom practice? The following are some primary take-aways for literature teachers from this voluminous body of research.

What Literature Teachers Can Learn from Research on Reading

- Make cognitive strategies visible to all students. Introduce your students to the idea that they have a tool kit of strategies that will help them create meaning as they read texts. As we discuss in Chapter 5, this approach is especially helpful to struggling readers.

- Use think-aloud protocols to promote metacognitive awareness. In other words, have students talk about what they are doing as they are doing it. Olson, Schoenbach et al., and Wilhelm offer textured examples of how think-alouds make "strategic knowledge visible and available to students and heightens their emotional and cognitive engagement" (Olson 28). For example, students can read a short text out loud and offer commentary on their reading as they read, naming what might have symbolic importance, articulating points of confusion, and predicting outcomes.

- Incorporate explicit teaching of skills within the context of literature instruction. For example, when you ask students to predict what might happen at the end of a novel or short story, let them know that they are using a cognitive strategy to enhance their reading. Similarly, if you use literature circles, note that each role—connector, summarizing, investigator—is an animation of a particular cognitive strategy.

- Consider the textured lessons of sociocultural research by acknowledging that reading is a social act nested within other social acts. Let students talk freely in a variety of ways about what they are reading and how they are reading. Invite them, for example, to bring their out-of-school reading into the classroom. Offer more opportunities for choice in what they read. Roam around your students as they are reading (Atwell, *Reading Zone*) to glean more insight into their reading process. Offer opportunities for students to create their own reading groups, constructed by mutual interests and not by perceived reading ability.

- Reconsider your literature curriculum in light of the diversity of your students. Ask yourself whose story is being heard, whose voice is being represented. Use contemporary short story collections or writing from magazines to bring new and diverse voices into your curriculum.

In the next chapters, we build on this knowledge base about reading research as we consider, through the eyes of a literature teacher, several important components of reading. We'll look at the challenges we face as we encourage struggling readers, we'll delineate ways of incorporating reading instruction into our literature classrooms, we'll explore the possibilities afforded by new literacies, and we'll consider the enactment of gender in reading practice. First, however, we tackle the teaching of literature head-on as we reconsider what a text actually is—and why rethinking our definition of text matters. We also explore the ways in which, at its heart, teaching literature *is* teaching reading. By weaving more explicit reading instruction into our literature classrooms, we can enhance our students' engagement with literature as well as their literacy skills.

What Is a Text? Real-World Literacy and Reading Instruction

Chapter Three

Who's Literate Now?

Suppose you came across this text:

> ! R u kidn me? OMG U r 2 funny!
> Dont 4get 2 tell ur frens. IMHO its xlnt.
> R u goin? PLMK. G2G.

What judgment would you make about the literacy skills of its creator? It seems that messages like this one have people screaming "Crisis!" With apologies to REM, it's the end of the word as we know it, and we don't feel fine. But what's really going on here?

Most text messages look more like plain English than this, but what you see here represents some of the ways in which an old orthography bends to meet a new technology. The symbols are creative, fast, and—at least to the initiated—mostly self-explanatory. What looks to baby boomers like a series of bad personalized license plates is in fact a form of literacy now in use and in constant formation. This is exactly the kind of thing that English teachers should be excited about, but instead, for many, it foretells a crisis. How can this be possible?

It seems that many adolescents today come to the printed word with different experiences that help them to read, decode, and construct texts spontaneously. Many teens have been socialized to think about text messages as having an immediacy of meaning, intuitive decodability, and no need for anything like a life span. They provide freedom of creativity in an error-free zone. The devices that carry these texts are everywhere, allocated one each to an entire generation, or so it seems. The phenomenon seemingly comes without conventions, without manners (like so many other social behaviors), and without a rhetoric that corporate America can sell. Yet these messages are texts—both through their literal name and how they function. They do everything that texts—in the way most of us traditionally know the term—are supposed to do. And like other newly invented texts, such as Twitter and inserted emoticons, they bend all the conventions to which we have grown accustomed, and this leaves us with a crucial question: what *is* a text and how do these new ways of communicating fit into our larger understandings of texts as a whole? It seems as though the whole phenomenon of text messaging is simply too big to ignore, and, interestingly, seems an appropriate metaphor for our expansion of the notion of texts at large. Even a quick Google search yields dozens of text message lesson plans. None, however, seems quite as well conceived as the lesson I observed in an urban high school classroom.

Romeo to Juliet: ILU

In Elizabeth Martinez's ninth-grade literature class, the students are reading *Romeo and Juliet*. Elizabeth chooses this play almost every year, in part because she knows that her students will see their own shadows sweeping across the play as they read it. She wants them to understand that Romeo and Juliet are, in fact, much like them. So this year she begins her class a little differently. She invites her students to bring out their cell phones if they have them—the same phones that she has admonished them in the past to keep turned off and safely stowed away—and place them on their desks. After doing a quick inventory of phones, she assigns the students to collaborative groups of four students each.

Elizabeth then explains the day's assignment. Having read act 2, scene 2 (the famous balcony scene) for today's discussion, they are to open their copies of the play to that scene and recall the conversation between the two title characters. Their next task is to construct a text exchange between the two, imagining that the conversation is set in the present day. She requires them to have at least five conversational exchanges and to hold to the general substance of the scene. She has had her students translate the text into modern English in the past, but they have had trouble converting Shakespeare's language into their language. Today's translation, surprisingly, seems easier to accomplish.

At the end of the exercise, the students write their exchanges on the board to share them with the class. Each group explains its translation and describes how it captures the gist of Shakespeare's dialogue. Finally, the whole class chooses what it thinks are the best exchanges from each group and completes the scene in miniature. At the end of today's class, they can think of themselves as text playwrights. Elizabeth, meanwhile, has bridged the gap between texts created outside of school and texts from the inside.

For the students, this exercise provides both fun and insight. They imagine ways to translate Shakespeare's language not just into modern English but also into a genre that they own. Here is one typical exchange they created:

Romeo:	WAN2TLK?
Juliet:	YTLKIN2ME?
Romeo:	Fosho! U R gr8t!
Juliet:	U 2!
Romeo:	U R gr8ter! LOL! Hot4U
Juliet:	YYSSW (Yeah, Yeah, Sure, Sure, Whatever)
Romeo:	Swear2God!
Juliet:	G2G POS (Got to Go. Parent over Shoulder)
Romeo:	BBFN TTYL (Bye bye for now. Talk to you later.)
Juliet:	BCNY SIT X (Be seein' ya. Stay in Touch. Kiss.)

Shakespeare it's not, but Elizabeth never intended the text exchanges to come out in iambic pentameter. What she did intend with this lesson was for her students to connect Shakespeare's language to their own.

In the end, her purpose in the exercise was not to have her students create art, but rather to get them to see the possibilities that language affords and the ways in which it works in different settings and toward different purposes. As *Adolescent Literacy: An NCTE Policy Research Brief* suggests, Elizabeth is building a bridge between her students' everyday literacy practices and the literary discourse of the classroom. She knows, as the brief reminds us, that her students are likely to be more engaged if she incorporates her students' out-of-school literacy practices into her literature lessons. By doing do, she simultaneously reaffirms the relevance of Shakespeare's text as well as validates the importance of their own textual constructions.

What Is a Text?

There was a time when talking about texts meant talking about well-defined documents: printed material constructed for specific purposes, edited professionally for accuracy and clarity, and presented in conventional genres. Today, our definition of a text has expanded greatly. Films and television programs are considered texts, as are webpages, photographs, musical compositions, advertisements, jokes, news stories, and pieces of art. Within the study of discourse analysis, even conversations are considered texts. The contexts within which we read texts are academic, cultural, commercial, legal, personal, religious, and social. Their intentions are aesthetic, scientific, persuasive, and social. And because our students encounter texts in myriad forms and vast numbers every day, contemporary literacy education needs to encompass the study of all of these artifacts. This is precisely what *Adolescent Literacy: An NCTE Policy Research Brief* refers to as multiple literacies: "Adolescents need bridges between everyday literacy practices and classroom communities" (p. 15).

Today's expanding notion of text requires a lot of different skills from all readers. And as literature teachers, we can use both the existence of multiple and varied texts and the questions of genre, contexts, and intentions of these texts to teach certain reading skills that will help our students become stronger and more savvy readers. The use of those varied texts helps build those bridges between "everyday literacy practices and classroom communities." In addition, when we offer our students a variety of texts, we help expand their literacy repertoire, enabling them to read and interpret meaningfully in a wide spectrum of textual encounters, both in and out of school. This makes our literature classrooms lively sites of unexpected reading instruction. Perhaps more important, our students become better prepared to engage in multiple 21st century literacies.

Reading Real-World Texts

Consider this headline and lead from the *Weekly World News*, a grocery store tabloid:

PALIN BAGS A BIGFOOT

WASILLA, AK – Records and eyewitnesses have come to light that prior to announcing her candidacy for the Vice Presidency, Sarah Palin shot a Bigfoot from a helicopter. A government helicopter was seen flying low over the Chugach National Park with what witnesses described as "a sexy librarian shooting out the side." Employees at a local bait shop report seeing a similar woman only hours before carrying an infant in a camouflage Baby Bjorn.

By the nature of its form, this text purports to be a news item, but its presence under a tabloid banner leads most readers (at least implicitly) to ask a series of questions. What is its intention? Is it really news? Is it entertainment? Is it permissible to fabricate stories if one assumes that readers understand the conventions of this genre and enter into the text knowingly? (This is, in fact, a parody of a news story.) How does one discern whether such a story purports to have truth-value? Does the publication make normal assumptions about the competency of its readers, assuming them to be suspending disbelief for the sake of entertainment, or does it actually think that readers are credulous enough to believe such a story? Could this headline be nothing more than a shameless vehicle for the transmission of advertising, or does it actually have a satiric intent as it critiques the apparent incompetence of legitimate news sources in judging newsworthiness? More important, how do we apply the rules of literacy to our consumption of such a text, especially given the rampant relativity of truth in the postmodern world?

Tabloids like *Weekly World News* (*WWN*) might actually prove useful for teaching literacy practices. The *WWN* tagline—"Don't believe everything you read, unless you read it here at www.weeklyworldnews.com"—is only half comical, and good readers have to recognize the funny half. But just as I modeled earlier, before our students can begin to evaluate any text, they must be able to discern the text's purposes: the intentions of its creators, their desired responses, and their ideological premises. Students must know how to read the context into the text itself, knowing, for example, that news media today are a site of political advocacy and entertainment as well as a source of information. Today's students must be able to recognize social assumptions and cultural presuppositions and must be aware that such cognitive operators are ubiquitous and inescapable. In other words, they must read both into and out of the text, understanding that the text itself, while it clearly has intention, only finds meaning in the act of being read.

For the most part, literate people read texts in the same way that they "read" people. They recognize the motivations behind words and actions, such as the ironic intent of the story from *WWN*. They are cognizant of political and personal agendas. They know that people and texts alike invariably ask us for something: our trust, our money, our belief, our support, our goodwill, or our compliance. They assume that people put on their best faces in public when they desire a positive response. By this definition, *reading* is something well beyond decoding. It is an ability to discern intention, desire, and influence in the messages we encounter—and this way of thinking about reading is central to the work of a literature class.

Defining a "Text"

Literacy traditionally has been defined as the ability to read and create written texts. More recent definitions, though, attempt to encompass the purposes of literacy within its definition. For example, the United Nations Educational, Scientific, and Cultural Organization (UNESCO) defines the term this way: "'Literacy' is the ability to identify, understand, interpret, create, communicate, compute, and use printed and written materials associated with varying contexts. Literacy involves a continuum of learning to enable an individual to achieve his or her goals, to develop his or her knowledge and potential, and to participate fully in the wider society" (UNESCO).

In contemporary terms, a text is an object that can be studied. It is typically bound in some way to an event, a form of expression, or simply by conventional labeling: everything that occurs between the title and "The End." Under definition, a text can be as short as a single-line poem or as large as a novel, possibly even consisting of many books, as in the case of the Bible. No matter how we define it, though, our recognition of a *text* creates an expectation that we are looking at a unified whole, something self-contained, and often with inherent rules and expectations.

For example, we can think of texts as stable or volatile. If we know, for example, that texts like webpages are dynamic, then we can take care to limit our assumptions about them to the time and manner in which we access them. A Shakespeare play is subject to editorial presentation, for example, based on differences between folio and quarto versions, but we still think of these texts as stable.

While we know these truths about texts, not all of our students do. Thus it is important for us to examine these several possibilities for defining texts with our students before setting out guidelines or expectations for reading them. For our purposes in English language arts, a text is generally written, and thus stable, at least at any given point in time. At least this is the kind of text that our understanding of "literacy" is built to encounter.

How an Understanding of Text Helps with Critical Reading and Practical Literacy

If we think of literacy as a set of strategies for creating meaning out of texts and the high school English class as a space in which this can happen, at some point we might ask what the reach of any such strategy would be. Do we use the same set of interpretive strategies to create meaning for a piece of sudden fiction and a software manual? If not, then in what ways are these strategies different? And how do we, as English teachers, help students learn how to use these strategies? Studying these interpretive strategies as linked to particular texts—making visible the underlying characteristics and qualities of particular texts—can help students learn that reading texts well means understanding how these texts work.

Defensive reading strategies, for example, constitute one form of literacy associated with ostensibly factual information. When readers understand the psychology of text creation—for example, the use of slanted language in news reporting—they take additional care before drawing conclusions or giving in to the perspective of a news story. Consider these two actual headlines from different newspapers reporting the same story:

Israelis kill 8 in Gaza raid (*St. Petersburg Times*)
8 Arabs die in battle to save weapons tunnel (*Miami Herald*)

Many people would read the first headline as having an anti-Israeli slant, whereas the second seems to place culpability with the Palestinians, who are referred to here by the more inclusive label "Arabs." To recognize these distinctions, though, young readers need to develop sensitivity to the uses and intentions for word choice and sentence construction.

For example, our understanding of lexical entailment tells us that the word *kill* includes intention on the part of the subject, whereas the word *die* leaves open the possibility that these eight deaths were not intended. Likewise, because the subject position of the sentence is the "focus position," our attention in the first headline is drawn to what the Israelis did, whereas the second sentence focuses our attention on what happened to the Arabs. In addition, the adverbial prepositional phrases create vastly different meanings. In the first, Israelis are depicted undertaking a "raid," whereas in the second Arabs appear to be defending clandestine access to weapons. In each case, the reader is seemingly led toward a preferred interpretation by the message created as a headline.

Further, each headline acts as a priming device. If the headline is successful in creating an initial interpretation of the action being reported, then the story that follows will most likely be read through an interpretation consistent with the idea in that headline. Because we are conditioned to be consistent—in the ways that we think, the ways that we feel, and the ways we feel about what we think—each headline has remarkable potential for shaping the meaning of the story that follows. When we add to this consistency the recognition that we will probably choose to read a story or pass it by based on our initial belief about what the story offers to tell us, we see an even greater need for the development of critical reading skills.

Teachers can foster this awareness by presenting differing accounts of the same news stories, like those found in the contrasting headlines earlier. Depending on the source of the story (Fox News vs. MSNBC, for example), the writer's ideological orientation, or the location of a story (front page vs. op-ed page), we expect the characterizations of a single event to take on nuanced differences. One exercise teachers can employ is the presentation of a story without identification of its source, its author, or its context. Opposing viewpoints, for example, are frequently available on op-ed pages of daily newspapers. The students then can identify what biases, attitudes, or other intentions they think these stories include, based on the specific features of language the stories contain. When the teacher later reveals the background of the story to the students, they can make connections between language in the media and political points of view.

Some English teachers might argue that this kind of exercise is outside the purview of our work, especially in a time of standards and curricular mandates. I disagree. Using this kind of exercise not only focuses on the multiple kinds of texts that exist in the world but also can serve as a precursor to the approaches to reading we want students to use for any kind of texts—including literary texts. For example, the skills students hone in this exercise come in handy when we consider unreliable narrators like Huckleberry Finn or Arnold Spirit, the protagonist of Sherman Alexie's *The Absolutely True Diary of a Part-Time Indian,* or when we read texts with political undertones from *Animal Farm* to *Persepolis.*

What Do Texts Do?

In preparing lessons on real-world literacy, we might start with the assumption that all texts are intended to do something, both for those who create them and those who receive them. Messages capture the gamut of human motivations: belief, desire, hope, vision, and knowledge, to name a few. Linguistic texts, then, are better seen as embodied thoughts rather than disembodied messages. A poem, for example, while it might sit dormant on a page for centuries, nonetheless embodies the desire of the poet to express a new vision of the world, to bring about enjoyment and insight, and to make sense of human experience. Similarly, any reader who animates that poem is bound to blend new images with prior experiences, to delight in the beauty of its expression and in the satisfaction of new awareness, and to gain an expanded appreciation of familiar things.

In similar ways, even the most mundane texts connect with our emotions. News stories might pull at our fears. Instruction manuals are designed to bring us to the satisfactory completion of a task. Hobby magazines cause us to reflect on the enjoyment of personal interests. For those who like food, new recipes offer the promise of culinary delight. No matter what we read, we react to it, and in this awareness is a lesson for the literature classroom. The full gamut of human experiences is available to those who read literature.

Texts also operate upon our expectations. When we encounter writing of any given kind—a novel, a play, a news story, webpage—we expect it to do something. We expect news to inform us, a tragedy to purge our emotions, a novel to absorb us in vicarious experience. Of course, it is our transactions with texts that make them do things, but it is our expectation that they will do what texts of their kind are designed to do. If they fail to deliver their implicit promise, we deem it to be the fault of the text and not of our interaction with it. For this reason, the better we understand a text—both the text type and the content—prior to our experience of it, the better the chance that we will find satisfaction in it. This is consistent with one of the major findings of *Adolescent Literacy: An NCTE Policy Research Brief*, which underscores the importance of guided student choice: "Student-chosen tasks must be supported with appropriate instructional scaffolding" (xii).

If, for example, a teacher chose to read *Persepolis* with her classes, she'd need to offer some scaffolding around both the structure as well as the content of the graphic novel. First, students would need to explore the genre of the graphic novel and the ways in which it is both similar to and different from traditional comic books. One might then proceed to exploring visual representations of narrative by introducing the concepts of storyboards. After viewing a storyboard for films or even commercial advertisements, students, in small groups, could create graphic representations of texts the class has already read. Such activities ready them for the "reading" of a text like *Persepolis* with a format rarely encountered in high school literature classrooms.

In terms of content, a teacher might then provide students with some significant background into Iran's political past, particularly the unrest of Iran's Islamic revolution in 1979. This can be done through outside reading, which would also serve to incorporate informational texts into the literature classroom, something we literature teachers often need to do more of. One could also assign the gathering and presenting of background knowledge through collaborative groups, I-Search, or traditional research papers.

Then, as students read, teachers might offer ways of reading *Persepolis* through critical lenses of gender (Appleman, *Critical Encounters*, 2nd ed.) or cultural studies (Conners). These lenses focus on the social and political contexts of the world in which the text was written and how the world of the texts either reflects or resists the realities of that world. For *Persepolis*, that means students would focus on issues of power, gender, religion, and politics, and the intersection of all of those factors.

Finally, a critical viewing of the film version of the book and a discussion of how the two differ as texts could provide an excellent cumulative activity for engaging students in critical inquiry with a variety of texts.

Instruction in classic as well as contemporary literature should also be scaffolded. For example, before assigning Steinbeck's *Of Mice and Men*, teachers could provide scaffolded instruction for a variety of different approaches to the novel. To focus on the historical elements of the novel, students might complete modest research projects about migrant farmworkers in the 1930s. To focus on the political aspects of this work, students might be introduced to Steinbeck's belief in the utility of literature to promote social change by familiarizing themselves with the significance of *The Grapes of Wrath* and *In Dubious Battle*. Students might also consider the text through the literary lenses of gender and Marxism, to bring the portrayal and the struggles of the characters into sharper relief. Finally, teachers might want to introduce themes of friendship and the American dream though prereading activities that build on those ideas, so that when they encounter them in the text, the students already have the foundation for an interpretation.

What Do Texts Reveal about Their Authors and about Us?

The human element of textual analysis is one that we sometimes consider late, if at all, in the teaching of reading. Texts are more than objects; they are the expressions of their authors and the constructions of their interpreters. There is creativity on both ends of the textual transaction. In quite direct ways, texts represent the activity of the human mind. If we keep this idea in front of us as we read, suddenly reading becomes more interesting, more natural, and often more fruitful.

Cognitive scientists would tell us that each human mind is a closed system. By *mind* we mean the activity of the brain, and each brain resides within a body, safely encased in a shield of bone. The only way for ideas to get out and to find their way to other human beings is by way of representations: body language, facial and physical gestures, and, most frequently, language. In language, some *signified* thing, in Saussure's terms, becomes represented by a *signifier*, a sound image that we recognize as a sign, and in this way ideas pass from one person to another. As we assemble these signifiers into complex constructions, we create texts, and when we write these texts we preserve them and enable their broad and asynchronous transmission.

There is a temptation to see these texts as something divorced from the processes that created them, but when we give in to this temptation, reading becomes less engaging, less human. A simple reminder, then, keeps us engaged: there is always a person on the other end of a text. Because that person cannot give us direct access to an idea, she or he engages in a creative act of language. Linguists like Noam Chomsky and psychologists such as George Miller have commented that most sentences we speak, if they are more than a few words in length, are probably sentences that we have never spoken before, and they may well be sentences that no one has uttered before in the history of our language. Such is the degree of creativity in the creation of texts.

Any occasion for reading, then, provides an opportunity to explore the creativity of a text, no matter how mundane it may seem on the surface. We say, for example, that texts have voices, and that those voices are accomplished by art-ful choices of diction and syntax. Texts create moods, convey feelings, construct complex ideas, relate human events, and give pleasure by their beauty. They do this because they are forms of human expression. Even the weakest student essays we receive take on new significance if we keep this in mind. Someone is trying to talk to us, perhaps in a manner they do not yet understand, in forms they have not yet mastered, and in structures they cannot yet control. If we recognize the human be-ing on the other end of that text, though, we will address it differently.

Recognizing and naming that voice in the text is a central part of what litera-ture teachers do with their students, and it is a move that helps our students be-come better readers. As literature teachers, we want our students to hear the voices of the characters in the text. From the iconic voice of Holden Caulfield in *Catcher in the Rye*; to Steve, the troubled protagonist of Walter Dean Myers's *Monster*; to the deceased adolescent narrator in Alice Sebold's *The Lovely Bones*, teachers can help students hear the voices in the text in several ways, such as having them:

- Write papers from a character's point of view, including a meta-analysis of how the paper exemplifies the character's traits and speech of the character;

- Read aloud, focusing on the appropriate tone and emphasis of a character's voice;

- Role-play, which requires an internalization of the character's qualities and an ability to spontaneously animate them; and

- Place characters in different contemporary situations and predict how they might respond.

Implications for Our Classrooms

Schools have historically ignored texts that don't seem scholastic in nature. We may teach our students to deal with a variety of *legitimate* texts, but this criterion of legitimacy may cause us to ignore what could turn out to be a host of literacy practices in the future. On the one hand, of course, we want students to know and emulate the practices of Standard Written English. On the other hand, texts of other sorts may eventually play a large role in the lives of future citizens. For all we know, the conventions of today's text messages could become the new standard—or they could fade into the past, only to elicit an occasional nostalgic chuckle, like the speech of Valley girls made famous by Moon Zappa.

There is another reason, though, for considering this broader canon of popu-lar texts: they teach us how literacy conventions change in response to perceived public need. While it is within the purview of schools to validate the forms and kinds of texts that our larger society sees as *legitimate*, and while schools have for too long held to a prescriptive path in the teaching of language, the examination of new textual forms offers numerous opportunities for students to explore the ways in which texts work. The intuitive nature of text messages, for instance, makes these texts terrific examples not only of textual adaptation but also of changes in communicative behaviors.

If there is a gap in our current English language arts curricula, it is in the teaching of language itself. We need to focus our students' attention on more than the manifestations and sanctioned representations of language. We need to acknowledge for ourselves and make clear to our students that languages are dynamic. Preparation for their futures means preparation for change, and texts are bound to change in an era dominated by mass media and new media. In addition, the inclusion of new media texts in our curricula is by extension an inclusion of our students. Instead of teaching them the conventions of a literate world into which they may one day enter (and which may change even before they arrive), we can ask them to explain the texts that they create.

As *Adolescent Literacy: An NCTE Policy Research Brief* points out, if we make visible and validate the workings of their own literacies, our students will be more likely to engage successfully in academic literacies. We need to acknowledge our students' expertise in manipulating many different kinds of text. We can do this by incorporating digital technologies in our classroom through wikis, webpages, and even classroom-based Facebook pages or Twitter. (How engaging would it be to create character tweets!) We need to offer students opportunities to "bring the outside in" (Kadjer) by helping them find connections between the literature that we read and the texts with which they are most comfortable, such as magazines or websites. In particular, we need to broaden our definition of what a text is so that the texts of our students' lives become fodder for our literature classrooms in rich and valuable ways. Thus, as we consider the subject of the next chapter, teaching reading as we teach literature, it is important to keep these multiple literacies and our expanding notion of texts in mind.

Elizabeth Martinez, the teacher in the opening vignette of this chapter, did precisely that. She incorporated text messaging into her literature lesson on the most "academic" of all writers, William Shakespeare. In doing so, she tried to bridge the divide between the textual world of her students and the textual world of traditional literature classrooms. Her motivation is not simply to *cover* a canonical writer but to find ways to hook even her nonengaged readers. If we are indeed going to begin to teach reading as we teach literature, then we need to incorporate these multiple literacies and varied texts into our literature classroom. By doing so, we will not only hook nonreaders but we will also better serve all of the adolescent readers in our classrooms. Chapter 4 explores how we can teach reading as we teach literature in even more detail. In fact, as you'll discover, you're doing it already!

Teaching Reading and Teaching Literature

Chapter Four

Teaching Reading in the Literature Classroom

You already read my confession in Chapter 1. I am a literature teacher who, until very recently, thought that teaching literature and teaching reading were very different things. What was I thinking?! Maybe it's because I always taught at the high school or college level. Maybe it's because I was so infatuated with my literature lesson plans that I didn't always see the struggling readers in front of me. Maybe it's because I didn't want to see what I didn't know how to address, but I always assumed that it was a given that my students could already read, and all I needed to do was to have them *interpret*. In other words, reading was what they already knew how to do in order to do what I wanted to teach them.

Now, however, my perspective is completely different. To heed the call of concern of reports such as *Adolescent Literacy: An NCTE Policy Research Brief*, teachers of literature must reconsider their role as teachers of reading, which is, of course, the central focus of this book. My resolve to consider ways to incorporate the teaching of reading into the teaching of literature is informed by the growing body of literacy research that we reviewed in Chapter 2, by our collective redefinitions of what exactly constitutes a text in the midst of our consideration of 21st century literacies that I wrote about in Chapter 3, and, perhaps most of all, by my memories of all the adolescent readers whose learning needs I may have inadvertently sacrificed in the name of a canonical book that I felt I had to make sure that all students read. Yet this assertion that reading instruction should occur in the literature classroom raises all sorts of questions.

What exactly do we mean by *reading*? Is *reading* different from *reading literature*? What makes merely *reading* different from *reading well*? If reading takes place on a variety of levels and entails a diversity of skills, how do we determine who is actually *reading* and who is doing something less than reading? And, given the issues raised thus far, how do these questions connect to what we know about reading, research, adolescent literacy, and textual considerations?

One of my colleagues, we'll call him Jeff Johnson, framed this problem very nicely when he described his students' initial reactions to E. E. Cummings's poem, "anyone lived in a pretty how town." "What is this?" one student named Eric asked, initially baffled by the very first stanza, with its unusual syntax and unorthodox word choice:

> anyone lived in a pretty how town
> (with up so floating many bells down)
> spring summer autumn winter
> he sang his didn't he danced his did

Eric's first response, upon encountering this poem, was to exclaim, "I can't read this." When Eric says this, does he mean the same thing by *reading* that we mean? What did Eric expect that he was supposed to be able to do with this poem? Or was it a question about what he thought the poem was supposed to do when he read it? After checking with Eric about the nature of his difficulty, Jeff concluded that Eric had read the poem without difficulty, if we think of reading simply as the act of decoding the letters into recognizable words. However, while Eric could read the words of the poem, he still didn't seem to understand the poem at all. The question for Jeff (and for us) is this: was Eric *reading* the poem or not?

This question mirrors a larger question that literature teachers frequently ask: what does it mean to be *literate*? Depending on the context of the conversation, this word has at least two different meanings. The first and most common meaning describes an ability to decode and discern meaning from written discourse. A second definition entails knowledge of a specific area of study or discipline. This second definition undergirds the concept of *cultural literacy*. To be "literate" is to be acquainted with works of literature or other valued cultural artifacts. Back in the day when we focused more closely on canonical works of literature, we were more likely to describe a "literate" person as one who has been acquainted with the canon. Even now, in the face of other essential goals, literature teachers typically strive to move our students toward this second manner of literacy. Still, before we can do this, our students must be competent in the first: They must be able to take meaning confidently from the written page. As we come closer to understanding the complexity of what reading is, we recognize that literacy entails not just the *what* of reading, but the *why* and the *how* as well (Jacobs 14).

Our developing knowledge of both adolescent literacy and reading instruction enters in here as well. We know that adolescents are engaged with all kinds of texts, both in and out of the classroom. As we discussed in Chapter 2, we know that even students who appear to be nonreaders are actually reading, and, as we discussed in Chapter 3, we know that different kinds of texts require different kinds of literacies. We know, too, that literature teachers are *literacy* teachers, and, as such, our responsibility is to help students read the world and the word. We also know that we are not fulfilling that responsibility as well as we should. And, despite the burgeoning and progressive research on out-of-school literacies, the place that we literature teachers can work toward improving the reading proficiency of all of our students is in the literature classroom.

Those of us who see ourselves as literature teachers, though, might feel uncomfortable if someone were to ask us, "So, *how* do you teach reading?" Our first answer might be that we don't teach reading, at least not per se. We teach things that *require* reading, even that depend on skilled and careful reading, but most of us would probably say we don't teach reading in that first sense of the word. That is the purview of reading specialists and early grades teachers. Too often we assume that by the time they get to us, students have the prerequisite skills to know what a text *says*, and that once they possess that ability we can teach them how to do things with reading—like attempting to say what a text *means*.

As we attempt to locate ourselves and our work, then, we have to ask a series of questions. What do our students read for? To what purposes, in other words, do they put reading? Toward those ends, what does reading require of them? And finally, what does it mean to read well? As I've suggested throughout this book, while reading and literary studies have frequently been viewed as different camps in literacy education, theirs is not a dichotomous relationship. Good reading practice is essential to successful literary interpretation, and thus teachers of literature consistently build on and reinforce the foundation that reading teachers in early grades have established.

Literature is both a purpose for reading and a site for improving reading skills. The beauty of literature is that it provides opportunities to encounter reading of many kinds in texts that encompass diverse voices and cultures and offer myriad examples of the concepts and structures that shape our understanding of the world. As I discussed in Chapter 3, the acknowledgment of those different text types and our consideration of what a text is changes our understanding of our students' literacy needs; indeed, it changes our definition of what a text is. Our students are reading websites, Facebook pages, tweets, 'zines, graphic novels, young adult novels, billboards, magazines, advertisements, pamphlets, and, oh yes, poetry, short stories, and novels. Most important, though, we shift the meaning of the term *reading* when we locate it at this higher developmental level. In the literacy classroom, successful *reading* is a constellation of critical reasoning skills targeted toward knowledge construction. Reading is a way of encountering the world and making sense of it.

Literature: So Last Century?

Texts, as we established in the last chapter, are varied and constantly changing, especially in the world of 21st century literacies. Many people seem to wonder if there is a place in this world for what we consider literary texts. I would answer a resounding yes, and yet what we may need to think about as 21st century literacy teachers is *how* we are teaching these texts. What does it mean to teach literary texts in a time of 21st century literacy needs *and* a new emphasis on the importance of teaching reading?

There is widespread perception in the world outside of education that when we read we are primarily seeking information—that the desired outcome of reading is increased knowledge. This may be true in part, but it is only one facet of our engagement in written language. To date, there are approximately 50 million people who have Facebook accounts. MySpace, another social networking site, has reached 100 million accounts (though each is not owned by a separate user). Clearly, there is some enormous draw to these social networking websites. Their purpose is not to satisfy a need for information but rather to meet our desire to connect with other people like us. Reading on the Web, then, is more about engaging actively in the human experience than immersing oneself in human knowledge.

If engagement in human experience is that large a motivator of human action, then literature should hold significant promise as a source of human interest. Its beauty is found in its ability to convey this experience in as many ways as there are literary artists. Literature creates new ways of seeing and thinking about our experiences—through novel metaphors, unusual characterization, vicarious experience, harmonious sounds, historical importance, cultural rituals, social practices, political perspectives, satirical calls for social correction—and becoming more connected with the world around us.

Most important, if literature is a representation of human experience, and this experience is recorded for us within written texts, then literary reading can be both a means of reading development and a goal in itself. Purely as an activity, lit-

erature provides young readers with a wide array of texts from historically, cultur-
ally, and socially diverse circumstances. It promotes frequency of reading practice.
It enhances students' engagement in reading and gives teachers a way of assessing
that engagement. It enables students to build vocabulary by recognizing words
in context. It provides opportunities to explore the sounds of written texts and to
hear those sounds used toward a particular effect. It introduces readers to a variety
of genres and helps them understand what they ought to expect from each. And
finally, it gives students a reason to read: to be immersed in human experience.

In some form or other, then, literature makes use of all the skills that good
reading practice requires. And extended exposure to works of literature provides
students with a stock of new concepts and the words that represent them: words
that represent the myriad varieties of human experience. Exposure to a variety of
literary voices leads readers to internalize and interpret a larger repertoire of syntactic structures. Frequent readers are also exposed to a variety of devices for con-
veying meaning: *idiom*, *metaphor*, *metonymy*, *irony*, and *hyperbole*, just to name a few.
This list of terms, by the way, only provides names for linguistic phenomena with
which most speakers are already familiar before they begin school; they just don't
know (nor do most adults) that these language behaviors have technical names.
Further, it is not the naming of these phenomena that matters. It is the reader's
ability to recognize what these operations do that makes her or him a better reader,
and it doesn't matter whether this recognition is implicit or explicit. This ability
to name what it is that we do when we read is at the heart of the metacognitive
instruction that is described in Chapter 2 and will return to as we consider ways to
help the struggling reader. Literacy teachers, reading researchers, and cognitive
psychologists agree that if the implicit, automatic mental processes that constitute
the act of reading can be made visible to readers, their reading will improve.

What Does It Mean to Read Well?

While we can agree that improved reading is the goal for all of our students, we
may not agree on what kind of improved reading we are striving to achieve. What
does it mean to read well? In the age of standards, we might be tempted to say that
reading well means comprehending a passage and being able to correctly answer
questions about it. Yet reading well, for the literature teacher, entails much more
than that. This is a question that we might put to all of our students, especially
those who hope to teach one day.

Reading first requires decoding, but *reading well* entails much more. Like
writing, our references to *reading* include the strategies, the decoding activity
itself, an engagement of the imagination, the receipt of a specific message, and the
construction of an appropriate meaning for that text. The things that fascinate us

all about reading are those that happen after we decode the text—after we have acquired it. Once we have the text, we can begin to do things with it, and many of these activities are within the purview of what we call *reading*.

As teachers, we might ask ourselves, how do we know when students are reading well? Presumably, students who read well engage with reading in ways that readers who are less accomplished and less motivated don't. In an attempt to answer this question, here is a preliminary list of things that better readers of literature do when they *read well*:

- They visualize the content of the text.
- They empathize with narrators and characters.
- They predict the direction of a text.
- They hear the voices of people within literary texts.
- They recognize nuance in messages.
- They understand authorial intention.
- They identify the most important elements of the text.
- They construct meaning for themselves.
- They experience and appreciate beauty in human expression.
- They recognize adherence to and deviation from established cultural patterns like narratives or lyrics.
- They are cognizant of the ways in which texts reinforce social norms.
- They see reflections of other forms of human experience—both real and fictional—in literary texts.

Reading, then, aims at all of these objectives. To the extent that a reader can look at written text and visualize images within a real or imagined world, for example, *reading* is taking place as a fully activated process. Highly accomplished readers have almost direct access to the message that the text contains. This access is what causes us to physically start when reading a Stephen King novel or to cry at the culmination of *Of Mice and Men* or, for that matter, *The Lovely Bones*. Full access to the literary content of the text is the eventual goal of reading instruction.

As we all know, to arrive at this goal, readers must first accomplish an array of reading skills: decoding, word and concept recognition, grammatical assignment and sentence assembly, semantic understanding, pragmatic recognition of differing meanings for the same utterances in different contexts, and so on. Literary study provides a wealth of opportunities for instrumental practice as well as for its own artistic purposes.

Let's take a piece of literature that is frequently taught and see how we can use it to teach reading as we teach literature. In other words, let's see how a typical literature lesson could also become an effective lesson in reading instruction.

A Case Study in Teaching Literature as Teaching Reading: "The Things They Carried"

Tom has been teaching language arts for ten years in a diverse high school in the Midwest. He especially enjoys teaching American Literature, a yearlong required course. His third hour is a reflection of the diversity of his school, about half boys and half girls, 60 percent white and 40 percent students of color. The class includes a wide range of ability. As Tom puts it, "The class is neither Advanced Placement nor remedial; it's the mythical middle—just plain kids." I love when my methods students visit Tom's classroom, which he generously opens to us every year. They find his energy and twin passions for the students he's teaching and for the literature he's teaching them to be utterly inspiring.

Lately, Tom says, his classes have not been going quite as well as he wants them to. He's noticed a few things about his class that have caused him to reconsider his approach to teaching American literature:

- Lots of his students seem plugged in to numerous digital literacies, to the point that they sometimes seem distracted.

- Students also seem tuned in to world events, including the continuing wars in Iraq and Afghanistan.

- The males in the class, in particular, haven't been enthralled by the "oldies but goodies," whether they were culled from the literature anthology or from the stores of Perma-Bound books.

- Several students seem to be reading slowly and having some difficulty keeping up with longer pieces of text.

- Tom's been doing a lot of studying on gender and reading, a topic we discuss in detail in Chapter 6, and he wants to make certain that he chooses a text that reflects what he knows about the kinds of texts that engage male readers.

Text Choice

Given all of these factors, Tom decides to teach the short story "The Things They Carried" (1986) by Tim O'Brien. It's engaging, contemporary, and has a strong voice. Given how many of Tom's students are touched by war, it also has relevance to the lives of students outside of school. Many of them have family members and older class-mates who have been deployed to wars or who have experienced losses in previous wars.

"The Things They Carried" is currently widely taught either in its original form as a short story or as the first chapter of O'Brien's novel of the same name. In the story, O'Brien introduces the readers to the members of Alpha Company, a group of soldiers serving in Vietnam, through a descriptive cataloging of the things they carry with them in their backpacks. We learn, for example, that someone carries letters from his girlfriend, another a Bible, another photographs, another sap and a toothbrush. They all carry ponchos and bandages, helmets and boots.

Thus, we learn something about the universal experience of war as well as the individual experiences of each soldier.

As Tom prepares to teach the story, his mind is also on something else—his students' performance on state-mandated reading tests. Tom confides that his school, like so many others, is struggling with low test scores in reading on the required state exams. He and his fellow language arts teachers feel pressure, both from administrators and from themselves, to begin to address the students' performance in reading. To that end, Tom has attended some professional training focused on reading strategies and has been reading some of the literature that we cited in Chapter 2 and that will come up again during our discussion of the struggling reader in Chapter 5. "It's funny," he says. "I teach kids, and I teach them books, and I love it, but I didn't really know the first thing about how to actually teach them to *read* the books. It turns out that some of what I think I need to do to get them to interpret is what I need to do to get them to read. I just need to be more intentional about it." What follows is a brief peek into Tom's lesson to illustrate how teaching literature is teaching reading.

Motivation

Tom begins with a whole-class discussion on the current situations in Iraq and Afghanistan. The students, many of whom have been touched by war, are deeply engaged. What is evident is what Csikszentmihalyi as well as Smith and Wilhelm call *flow*, and Tom thinks hard about how to keep the discussion flowing. One way he does so is to follow up with a photo essay on war and a *Time* magazine article called "The Things They Carried," which actually looks at the things that contemporary soldiers carry, a direct tie-in to the text.

21st Century Literacy Connections

Tom knows from current research that his students engage in non-school literacies. He builds upon that by having students search for war-related blogs, YouTube videos on the Vietnam War, and informational websites that deal with the Vietnam War and its aftermath as well as contemporary military situations. In other words, Tom is trying to plug his classroom into the technologies that students use with ease. He even creates an assignment called "The Apps They Carried" and asks students to imagine what kinds of applications a soldier would need on her iPhone.

Tapping Prior Knowledge

Tom tries to draw on his students' prior knowledge, both of historical events as well as literary conventions. He knows that the American history courses his students take cover Vietnam and so he reintroduces some of the material that his history colleagues use. He also refers students to their well-worn glossary of literary terms to review some concepts that will be relevant to their reading of this story, such as genre, point of view, character, and tone.

Preteaching

Tom knows that good readers need to know what they are reading. "The Things They Carried" offers a unique opportunity to discuss genre, since it was indeed published originally as a short story but later became the leadoff story for a novel, which, like Hemingway's *In Our Time,* can be considered either a novel or a collection of short stories. Tom also understands the importance of preteaching vocabulary in context and offers his students the following words before they encounter the story: *napalm, gyroscope, ordnance, diddly,* and *hootch,* as well as a variety of military terms.

In fact, Tom creates an impromptu class assignment during which students create their own glossary of military terms and slang.

During Reading

Tom tries to keep things moving as students read the short story. Students read the story together in small groups, highlighting passages that they think are particularly significant. They fill out KWL's and write lists of questions they want the class to consider on the board. In addition to the vocabulary words that Tom supplies, students also make a list of unfamiliar words as they read.

Post-Reading Interpretation: Literary Lenses

One of the more significant trends in secondary literature instruction over the past two decades has been the introduction of literary theory into our English classrooms (Appleman, *Critical Encounters,* 2nd ed.). So that our students might see the possibility of multiple interpretations for any given literary text, teachers can introduce them to a variety of literary lenses, including feminism, Marxism, reader response, even deconstruction. Turning poetry, short stories, and novels different ways to refract different shades of meaning is what literary theory can do for our students. And, in fact, this approach toward seeing texts and worlds is also teaching reading—and is a perfect example of how literature teachers can provide reading and literature instruction at the same time. Using multiple lenses to view a piece of literature provides students with opportunities to read, to reread, and to discuss their varying interpretations.

Teachers, for example, could use the following lenses with "The Things They Carried":

Historical lens: This lens would situate the story firmly in the context of the Vietnam War and would ask students to consider the historical significance of the work in the context of American history.

Biographical lens: This lens would bring the life of Tim O'Brien, himself a Vietnam veteran, into sharper relief. Students could consider how their knowledge of the author's biography informs their textual interpretation.

Gender lens: In addition to looking at the presence or absence of women in O'Brien's work in particular and war stories in general, this lens enables students to consider the social construction of masculinity and how the concepts of war and soldier fit into that social construction.

Marxist lens: This lens would consider the political ramifications of the United States as a world power and how its capitalistic value system affects its decision to engage in war.

Reader response lens: This lens would encourage students to consider how their own and their families' experience and perspective on war as well as their own political sensibilities affect their reading and interpretation of the text.

Continuing the Flow

Tom feels that his students enjoyed the experience with the short story and offers them the opportunity to continue with the entire novel, *The Things They Carried*. He also suggests critical viewing of some of the following films that powerfully consider the effects of war: *Band of Brothers*, *The Hurt Locker*, *Coming Home*, *Platoon*, and *Full Metal Jacket*.

Conclusion: Literature Instruction and Reading Instruction

For most literature teachers, the lesson for "The Things They Carried" should seem very familiar. In fact, you might wonder what is new about this approach of teaching literature as teaching reading. In fact, that is exactly what Tom discovered. What we do as a matter of course in our literature classrooms—prereading activities, vocabulary, and strategies to enhance comprehension—are all moves, as my friend Michael Smith would say, that literature teachers make. What we need to do in our instruction is to be explicit about the ways these instructional moves engage our students not only in the process of interpreting literary texts but also in the processes of reading itself. Through his new emphasis on those reading processes within the context of his literature instruction, Tom is well on his way to teaching reading successfully as he teaches the literature he loves.

As with Tom's choice to teach "The Things They Carried," another key to addressing the issues of teaching reading successfully in literature classrooms lies in creating good matches between readers and texts. Vicki A. Jacobs argues that we need to know the location of adolescent literacy within the stages of reading. Leaving aside for the moment her important question about when adolescent literacy actually begins, we can first recognize that students at this age read and relate to texts differently from younger readers. Jacobs reviews the list of tasks that constitute what we call successful reading at the secondary level and beyond:

> They learn how to apply vocabulary comprehension and study skills to determine purposes for reading; make predications; locate main ideas; question, analyze, and synthesize text; navigate varied text structures; identify and clarify multiple points of view; acknowledge the effect of content on meaning; and draw on background knowledge and previous academic and life experience to construct meaning. (14)

This stage of reading, which Jacobs calls "reading for learning the new," is where secondary literature teachers most often find themselves. Within a developmental model of reading instruction, teachers of literature prepare their students not only to read within a specific discipline but also to read with a range of crucial purposes. Reading well entails far more than decoding the contents of a written page.

Our purposes for addressing reading directly and explicitly in literature classrooms grow out of a set of much larger needs. Of course we want students to engage with literary texts, but we want them to understand the purposes of literary reading as well. Jacobs summarizes the purpose of content-based reading beautifully: "If students are to acquire these advanced reading skills and become critical readers within their disciplines, then teachers need to go beyond assigning merely *what* to read by giving students explicit explanations about the *why* and *how* of their reading" (14).

Teaching reading as we teach literature is also the only way we can begin to effectively address the needs of the subject of the next chapter, the struggling reader. If indeed we are teaching students, not just literature, then we need to reframe and reconsider our instruction so that all students can engage productively with texts. In the next chapter, we reconsider literature instruction in the context of the struggling reader.

Chapter Five

To Read or Not to Read: Rethinking the "Struggling Reader" in the Literature Classroom

L et's be realistic. Suppose you do expand your literature curriculum to include the varied forms of texts that we discussed in Chapter 3. Suppose you do incorporate many of the ideas we offered in Chapter 4 that will enable you to offer explicit reading strategies for your students as you teach literature. Suppose you are as welcoming as you can be about the multiple literacies that students bring with them to school and you integrate those literacies into your literature classroom in an admirably twenty-first-century way. There will *still* be some students in your English classes who have trouble reading. What becomes the role of the English teacher in teaching reading to these students?

It's funny. During my entire career as a high school English teacher, I thought of myself as a teacher of literature, not reading. I can see now that the distinction, while understandable, was not only silly; it was counterproductive. After all, what did I think my students were doing with the literature I assigned? They were *reading* it, of course! My failure to identify myself as a teacher of reading was perhaps the most costly for the students in my class who were struggling with reading. Of course, as a conscientious teacher, I worked hard to meet the needs of all my students and was continually assessing their progress as well as their challenges. I referred the students who seemed to have significant reading difficulties to "specialists" who met with the students outside of the context of my classroom. I didn't know then what I know now—that all teachers of literature can integrate reading instruction in their mainstream literature classroom to better meet the reading needs of all students, including those who struggle with reading. Consider the following scene from a classroom I visited.

Reading Instruction in the Mainstream English Classroom

Sally Kerr's fourth-hour tenth-grade English class is a typical urban classroom, large and strikingly diverse in every way, including in reading ability. The students have just read Abraham Rodriguez Jr.'s "The Boy without a Flag," a contemporary story about a young Puerto Rican boy who disobeys school authorities by refusing to salute the American flag. Nearly every hand is raised, as every student clamors to join the discussion about whether the protagonist of the story has made the right decision. Sally skillfully guides her students into a Human Barometer exercise, during which all students stand and line up according to the strength and side of their position. This time, all students are able to participate because they have read, comprehended, and interpreted the story. Although the story is challenging, no student seemed to be left behind in Sally's two-day lesson around the story, not even David.

David has been labeled a struggling reader throughout his schooling experience. When his teachers began diagnosing reading abilities and grouping students on the basis of those abilities, David always found himself in the slow group. His parents thought that this was a bit odd since they didn't consider David to be a nonreader. He seemed to spend hours on his computer, reading websites, writing on social network sites, and searching for information. In addition, he often had his face in some sports or automotive magazine. Still, David's grades have been declining throughout high school, and all of his teachers have cited his "poor reading skills" as the source of his academic difficulty. During this particular literature lesson, however—one that revolves around a contemporary and sophisticated short story written for adults—David was engaged during every part of the lesson.

Sally provided a scaffolded reading experience (Graves and Graves; Appleman and Graves) for her students, a lesson framework that allowed her to plan a lesson specifically designed for this particular group of readers and this story. In the story, a Puerto Rican boy, influenced by his father's political identity as a Puerto Rican, refuses to recite the Pledge of Allegiance along with the rest of the students in his elementary school auditorium. Because of his refusal, he is sent to the principal's office and severely reprimanded. When his father arrives at the school, the boy is surprised that is father is angry and upset, rather than proud, at what he has done. The story concludes with a growing understanding between the boy and the father about what challenges they each face as they learn to be both Puerto Rican and American.

Sally began her lesson on "The Boy without a Flag" by having her students do a close reading of the Pledge of Allegiance. This close reading modeled the kind of reading strategies that all readers, not just struggling readers, need to engage in. She gave the students a glossed version of the Pledge of Alliance and they read through it together, line-by-line and word-by-word, to improve their comprehension. After reading and discussing the pledge, Sally asked each student to write his or her own pledge, one that was inclusive of everyone in the class. This activity not only foreshadowed a major theme and specific elements of the story they were about to read, but it also gave readers a personal link to the story itself. Sally then proceeded with two other prereading activities. First, she asked the students to write a collaborative poem with another student, completing the line "I am the ____ without a ____" to help set the tone of the story of a boy without a flag. Finally, to activate prior knowledge as well as personal experience, she asked the students to complete a word picture of their elementary school. Before the students began reading the story, Sally previewed all the vocabulary that she thought might be difficult or unfamiliar. She then passed out a storyboard (Olson 87) for students to complete in pairs.

The next day in class Sally asked students to summarize the story and identify places where they got stuck. She followed this summary with a whole-class sharing of the story maps. Then she concluded with two extension activities. First, she asked students to identify their positions both on reciting the Pledge of Allegiance in general and toward what happens in the story. As mentioned previously, she first conducted a human barometer, in which students lined up according to their positions on the question "Should the father have supported his son in his decision not to recite the pledge?" Finally, students completed a discussion web in which they tracked their responses to whether students should be required to recite the Pledge of Allegiance.

Through her careful planning and use of pre-, during, and post-reading strategies, Sally had ensured that David was both motivated and engaged. By planning meticulously and implementing a variety of instructional strategies that were designed to enhance student comprehension, she was able to bring David-the-struggling-reader along with the more proficient readers in his class.

Rethinking the Struggling Reader

Exactly what is a struggling reader? Here is an account by a leader in literacy education and reading specialist that raises the question:

> Kylene Beers was conducting an in-school study of struggling and resistant readers. And she was stumped. In front of Beers sat a seventh grader who never seemed to read, presumably because he didn't read well and didn't like trying. Or so Beers thought.
>
> "Actually, I love to read," he told her.
>
> "You're kidding me," she said. "Whenever I see you in class you're either doing your homework or sleeping." A budding gymnast, the boy told Beers that practice, school, and homework left him little time for reading.
>
> "I'm like those bulbs you plant when the weather is cool but don't expect them to bloom until the ground temperature warms," he said. "Those bulbs are dormant. That's what I am. I'm a dormant reader."
>
> "When I asked him to explain, he said that he was just waiting for the right time, and that meant when he had some time to turn to the books he had collected and wanted to read," she said.
>
> For Beers it was an important discovery because it shed light on the time crunch many children face and the ways in which it affects their ability to develop a habit of reading and in turn refine their reading skills. But perhaps her most important finding was this: The boy who appeared to be a struggling reader really wasn't one at all.
>
> Mike Knight, *Minneapolis/St. Paul Magazine*

For better or worse, educators as well as the public at large have used the term *struggling readers* to describe students who seem to be either not reading or unable to read at grade-level proficiency. Yet the definition of struggling readers is difficult to pinpoint, and the population of students to whom the term refers is contested. My adult reading group, for example, often begins its meetings with confessions of various kinds of our struggles with a particular text. It's useful for us as teachers to remember moments like those, to be mindful of what it feels like to *want* to understand a text but to struggle with it, despite our best efforts. As Beers writes, "Remember that *anyone* can struggle given the right text. The struggle isn't the issue; the issue is what the reader does when the texts get tough" (15).

Additionally, O'Brien, Stuart, and Beach point out that what we mean by *proficient readers*, clearly the opposite of *struggling readers*, has changed as readers are introduced to "new textual landscapes" (80). O'Brien and his colleagues warn us against a kind of either/or bifurcation in which readers are either struggling or they are proficient. Proficiency, they argue, is dependent upon text, context, and a host of other factors. Concurring in effect with Beers's observation, they write "'proficient' readers are not always proficient and struggling readers do not always struggle" (81).

A Serious Problem?

Given all this, what do we even mean by the term *struggling reader*? Johannessen and McCann consider struggling readers to be those who experience difficulty "in accomplishing the literacy tasks that are valued in schools and that influence social and economic mobility" (65). These authors remind us of the inextricable relationship between adolescent identity and the discourse communities in which they find themselves, both in and out of school. This is an important consideration to keep in mind when we label adolescents as struggling readers.

Yet despite the appropriate warnings about the inadequacy of the term, there is no doubt that much attention is given to the existence of struggling readers. Struggling readers do not merely appear in the discourse of federal reports; they are in our classrooms as well, often falling behind, not doing the assigned reading, lacking engagement and motivation in reading-based classroom learning, and doing poorly on both standardized assessments and district- or classroom-based assessments. And outside evidence supports the notion that many readers do struggle. As *Adolescent Literacy: An NCTE Policy Research Brief* states, "Less than half of 2005 ACT-tested high school graduates demonstrated readiness for college-level reading, and the 2005 NAEP reading scores for twelfth graders showed a decrease of 80 percent at the proficient level in 1992 to 73 percent in 2005."

There are as many negative statistics about struggling readers as there are federal reports. For example, in 2005, 50 percent of California fourth graders scored below the "basic" level of reading achievement set by the National Assessment Governing Board. According to the National Right to Read Foundation, 20 percent of high school seniors can be classified as functionally illiterate at the time they graduate. According to the *Reading Next* report, "approximately eight million young people between fourth and twelfth grade struggle to read at grade level" (Carnegie Corporation 3). Citing a number of statistics from a number of sources, *Reading Next* continues: National Assessment of Educational Progress testing indicates that the percentage of American children who are able to read well hasn't improved at all in the last 25 years; on international tests, America's twelfth graders rank last in advanced physics when compared with students in eighteen other countries; and one-third of all incoming college freshmen enroll in a remedial reading, writing, or mathematics class. These numbers are even bleaker, according to the report, in the inner cities and poor rural areas, where 68 percent of low-income fourth graders cannot read at a basic level. In fact, despite $120 billion in federal spending since 1965 to raise the achievement of poor children, a wide educational attainment gap remains between rich and poor students. Given the amount of research and federal funding spent on literacy education (some estimate it at approximately $10 billion), and given the training and dedication of the vast majority of language arts educators, one has to wonder why there are still so many struggling readers in our classrooms.

According to some, the root of this problem lies with our public education system. As we will explore further in Chapter 8, many adolescents experience the language arts curriculum as boring and irrelevant. It's not that Johnny can't read; he just doesn't want to read what we've assigned him. Nor is he interested in inauthentic post-reading assignments that often feel like busywork. Several recent explorations into adolescent literacy find that many of those adolescents who are struggling readers do read outside of school, but for specific purposes, often related to their continuing expression of identity and their location within a particular socially situated discourse community (Gee, *Social Linguistics*). Many adolescents are interested in reading texts that connect to their lives, offer useful and relevant information, provide opportunities for self-expression and self-discovery, and provide opportunities for authentic intellectual engagement.

More Than One Answer

Despite the complexity of the notion of the struggling reader, there has been considerable research designed to guide classroom teachers in their work with such students, research that is particularly useful to teachers who think of themselves first and foremost as teachers of literature. As Kylene Beers points out, although "there are no single answers," we do have some answers. We know that the explicit teaching of cognitive strategies, the inclusion of the multiple literacies in which adolescents engage, learner-centered inquiry approaches, and a reconsideration of what it is that constitutes a *text* are all indeed very helpful. And we have numerous authors, such as Kylene Beers, Cris Tovani, Stephanie Garvey, Kelly Gallagher, Carol Booth Olson, Jeff Wilhelm, and others, who provide some useful strategies for dealing with struggling readers. Michael Graves also has articulated some very useful strategies, using scaffolded reading experiences like the one illustrated in the opening vignette of this chapter.

At this point, it's important to remind ourselves that even if we consider ourselves to be teachers of literature rather than teachers of reading, we are, above all else, teachers of kids. Let's remind ourselves of what it's like to have a struggling reader in a literature class. He or she usually appears listless and distracted, not listening to or participating in the classroom conversations. How could he, if the text he hasn't read is the focus of the discussion? The student's lack of reading becomes apparent in all student learning activities, including tests, essays, and quizzes. Especially painful is what happens when the student is asked to join cooperative learning groups or even a quick pair-share, when he has nothing to say. Struggling with reading is costly to students, socially as well as academically and psychologically.

For the mainstream literature teacher, it is difficult to know exactly what to do for the struggling reader in our classroom, especially if we feel that our general English education teacher training hasn't prepared us to teach reading. Too often we press ahead with our lessons, with our struggling students falling further and further behind. If we are honest with ourselves, we tend to be more likely to pitch our instruction where it will benefit most students, and we are guilty of ignoring the struggling readers. We tell ourselves it's because we don't want to embarrass them with pullout strategies that isolate them and their reading difficulty. So instead we opt to do very little, perhaps hold a few individual conferences or even make a call or send a progress note home.

Regardless of the size of our literature classes, which admittedly are getting larger and larger, we cannot afford to ignore the struggling readers in our classroom. Their literacy issues will only worsen with each successive school year, and it is our responsibility to teach them. In the rest of this chapter, we'll review some approaches that may help.

Several things are important for the classroom English teacher to remember in considering how to integrate these targeted reading strategies into her existing curriculum. The first is that it is important not to isolate struggling readers or to ostracize them by spotlighting their difficulties or separating them with pullout instructional strategies. Many of the strategies articulated by the research we have mentioned here can be helpful and productive to readers of all ability levels. The Pygmalion concept has been around as long as George Bernard Shaw, and one of the most important things we need to recall is that our expectations and our language are among the most influential factors in determining a student's academic success. If we continue to label and treat struggling readers as such, we are perpetuating their identities as nonreaders. While reading struggles is a serious academic challenge that needs to be addressed, changing our language as well as our expectations is perhaps the first and most important thing we can do. For example, identifying students positively based on their reading interest can help even reluctant readers form reading identities. In an all-male book club I love to attend, I overheard a tenth-grade boy say, "We're readers, all right—we just like to read books with lots of action!"

Providing individual attention to readers within the context of the literature classroom is another important principle to integrate into our practice. One of the greatest benefits of strategies, such as think-alouds and other successful cognitive strategies, is that they require individual interaction between the reader and the teacher. Students who struggle with reading do not necessarily need to be pulled out of their mainstream literature classrooms, but they do need individual attention for diagnosis, practice, encouragement, and assessment. For example, I know several teachers, both at the middle and the high school levels, who require students to keep a weekly reading journal that looks something like Figure 5.1.

The teachers skim through the journals and then schedule regular meetings with kids, often during class reading time, to discuss reading strategies. Yes, this strategy requires both dedication and a time commitment, but it can really pay off in terms of providing every reader with individualized attention.

Literature teachers also will be happy to know that many of the reading strategies discussed earlier also benefit proficient readers in their reading and interpretation of literary texts. The incorporation of reading activities such as scaffolding,

---

Figure 5.1: Sample Page from a Weekly Reading Journal

```
                    Weekly Reading Journal
Name:
Period:
Text:
This week I read from page ___ to page ___ .
The most important line(s) I've read so far:



A passage I didn't understand at all is:



Here are two questions about the reading I'd like to ask you:



Here is one question about the reading I'd like to ask my
classmates:



One thing that might help me with my reading of this book is:
```

---

frontloading, and other activities into our mainstream literature instruction can improve our students' comprehension and encourage them in their interpretations of literature. For example, previewing strategies, KWLs, think-alouds, reading apprenticeships, and the kinds of cognitive strategies/reading apprenticeship approaches we discussed in Chapter 2 are all strategies that can be profitably used by other readers. Reading aloud is another good strategy for struggling readers that can be useful for all readers, even though it's a strategy that has its detractors—especially if it is used in such a way that it isolates or ostracizes those students who are struggling. Scaffolded reading, as mentioned earlier (Graves and Graves), is another example of a strategy that classroom literature teachers use to construct lessons that can be used with all students, regardless of their ability level.

How might these multiple strategies take shape in a literature classroom? Meet Jessica, a teacher in her sixth year at a diverse inner-ring suburban school. She teaches a mainstream literature elective, but she admits that she has several students within every class who might be identified as struggling readers. She is planning to teach *The House on Mango Street* by Sandra Cisneros and wants to incorporate some strategies to ensure the success of her struggling readers. Here's a brief peek at how Jessica incorporates some of the strategies we discussed earlier in this chapter.

The Struggling Reader at *The House on Mango Street*

Text Choice

To include her struggling readers, Jessica chooses a text with easy readability but complex themes and characters. She knows she can't always choose texts at this reading level, but she wants her struggling readers to experience some success with a whole-class novel. Other deceptively simple texts full of rich possibilities for teaching include *Montana 1948*, *The Old Man and the Sea*, *The Pearl*, *Monster*, *Bronx Masquerade*, and even *Of Mice and Men*.

Prereading

Jessica uses the story "Eleven" by Sandra Cisneros as an introduction to the novel. Using shorter fiction to help struggling readers get on board with longer pieces of text can be a profitable strategy, one that introduces all readers to the tone and style of the author, or what many reading teachers call "author's craft." She uses Google Maps to hone in on Esperanza's street in Chicago and talks a bit about Chicago's ethnic neighborhoods. She also preteaches some Spanish words, enlisting the help of her native Spanish speakers who embrace the opportunity to be an expert for once in their English class. She has students speculate on the significance of the translation of Esperanza's name, hope. Jessica also introduces a KWL chart so that students can track their growing knowledge as they read about Esperanza, her coming-of-age challenges, and the role poverty plays in her life and the life of her family.

During-Reading Think-Alouds

Because the book is in short chapters, it easily lends itself to opportunities for reading aloud. Jessica divides the class into small groups of four. Each group takes turns with one reader reading aloud, stopping after each passage, with each group member discussing their thinking processes and growing questions as they read. This way, Jessica protects some struggling readers from having to choose to read out loud if they do not feel comfortable doing so, but to still be able to experience the cognitive benefits of the think-aloud.

Readers Theater

Although the novel focuses on Esperanza, there are many different characters in the novel—including a number of male characters. Jessica assigns parts to her students, and they incorporate some lines from the text into an original readers theater. She assigns each student a single character to be in charge of, making sure that her struggling readers are assigned manageable but important parts. Jessica works with each group during class time to help them create their readers theater piece.

Multiple Literacies

Jessica then assigns her students a digital project, in which they can choose to create a Facebook page for Ezperana, tweets between characters, or text messages similar to the ones used in the *Romeo and Juliet* lesson we discussed in Chapter 4. In addition to being of high interest to all readers, these lessons are designed to pull in some of the male readers, something we'll discuss in more detail in the following chapter.

Post-Reading

Jessica asks her students to model the genre of the book by writing three short memoir chapters from their own experiences, linking the world of the text to their own and strengthening their knowledge of the textual properties of the novel by imitating them. She also has them do short evaluative writing of their experiences with the book. Specifically, Jessica asks students questions about vocabulary, flow, and their own level of engagement. In addition to creating a metacognitive conversation about their reading experiences, Jessica hopes this conversation will help her struggling readers as she will use this information to plan future literature lessons.

As with the strategies we discussed in Chapter 4, nothing in this lesson should feel completely unfamiliar to literature teachers. Jessica is simply being more intentional about reaching her struggling readers. In addition to these instructional strategies, here is a list of specific approaches as we reframe our work with struggling readers:

What Literature Teachers Can Do to Encourage Struggling Readers

- First, change the language of *deficient*. Perhaps, as in the story in the beginning of the chapter, students are not so much *struggling readers* as they are *dormant readers*.

- Next, try to assess the kinds of reading challenges that students are experiencing. It's important to determine the degree of difficulty the student is experiencing. What kind of reading problem is it? Is it about motivation or ability or perhaps a combination of both?

- As we discuss later in Chapter 8, reconsider the kinds of texts you are asking the student to read.

- Offer students choice. There may be a terrific alternative to the whole-class text that is not working well for a particular student.

- While it may be impossible, given our acute economic crisis, to garner the funding to significantly reduce class sizes, it still might be possible to find ways to work individually with those readers who are labeled as struggling. Using instructional aides or parents and community volunteers to provide another pair of hands, eyes, and ears in the classroom can help increase the chances that all students will receive individual attention from a knowledgeable adult.

- Creating partnerships with local colleges and universities can also be a good strategy. Most states require that teacher-licensure candidates across all subject areas receive training and practice in the teaching of reading. There may be an eager group of reading tutors ready to become part of your classroom.

- Use reading techniques that benefit all readers. Preteaching vocabulary, doing close reading, making connections between literature and students' life experiences—the kinds of activities that Sally Kerr used in our opening vignette—are all activities that benefit not only struggling readers but all readers.

Conclusion

While there are clearly readers who struggle in our classrooms, there is much that a teacher can do to help motivate, engage, and improve their reading skills. In seeking to address the needs of struggling readers, we may find that our literature classrooms are richer places for all readers. In their discussion of "adolescents who struggle," Johannessen and McCann suggest, "We need to create a new kind of classroom, a classroom that is inquiry driven and is not driven by teacher-centered instruction" (77). In that new classroom, struggling readers like David will be integrated, not isolated, into a kind of intentional literature instruction that will inevitably enrich the reading skills of all students, regardless of their reading ability. This classroom will be filled with dialogue and genuine inquiry activities, and it will incorporate texts and activities that bring students' out-of-school literacy into the classroom. In addition, the teacher will make "connections to students' out-of-school experiences and cultures as they model critical thinking strategies for their students and utilize various types of discussions to help students figure out a difficult reading passage before they are asked to make interpretations on their own" (71).

O'Brien and his colleagues contrast approaching reading as a discrete set of decoding skills with the more contextual and integrative approach that this chapter advocates. As we consider opportunities for struggling readers to become more proficient, think about their conclusion: "If educators work on reading as a set of social and cultural practices, situated within lessons designed to engage students, the horizon is almost limitless" (95). Those social and cultural practices that surround our teens certainly contribute to how some students are seen as struggling readers.

One particular subset of those practices connects to issues of gender—how the cultures surrounding boys and girls affect how they experience our literature classroom, our choice of texts, and our instructional activities, and how they might see themselves as readers. In the next chapter, we'll consider how literature teachers can incorporate our growing knowledge about the gendered nature of reading practices into our classrooms.

**Chapter
Six**

The Gender of
Reading in the
Literature Classroom

I n the last chapter, we explored some strategies for the struggling readers
who are present in all of our literature classrooms. For the most part, our
discussion of those struggling readers was gender-free. To be sure, both
male and female students sometimes struggle in our classrooms, and
both male and female students can become enthusiastic and engaged readers
of literature. Both male and female students are affected by many of the factors
that *Adolescent Literacy: An NCTE Policy Research Brief* points to as changes in
the landscape of adolescent literacy—changing technology, multiple literacies,
and new media. Both engage in nontraditional textual reading outside of class,
although some researchers might posit that there are gendered patterns in that
as well. According to sociocultural theory, as we discussed in Chapter 2, for both
boys and girls reading is socially situated; that is, it is mediated and determined
by social factors. In fact, our notion of our reading selves is socially constructed
by the expectations of parents, teachers, and peers. Yet in many ways, the literature classroom is the ideal place to consider the social construction of gender

as we read and discuss literary texts. In doing so, we may provide opportunities for our students, both male and female, to consider their own gendered roles and to resituate themselves as readers.

According to *Adolescent Literacy: An NCTE Policy Research Brief*, concerns for literacy do cut across the lines of ethnicity and gender. Recent findings by NAEP, for example, demonstrate that decreasing literacy scores are found among black and white students and both girls and boys (*Adolescent Literacy: An NCTE Policy Research Brief* xi). At the same time, though, most of the attention given to gender in the study of literacy attainment has been focused on boys, largely because of what we know about the importance of motivation in schooling and the academic dangers that its absence creates. On the whole, girls seem to be more motivated to participate in school-sponsored tasks, especially reading. It is crucial, then, that we find a solution to this problem of motivation if we hope to increase literacy gains among all of our students, including boys.

At the same time, however, an overemphasis on concern for boys minimizes the challenges that female adolescents face in our literature classrooms. For example, girls too often report that they feel excluded or marginalized in the class activities that support their reading. Traditional classroom settings tend to favor the more aggressive and risk-taking styles of male communication. While girls are socialized to be cooperative in discourse, boys are socialized to compete for attention, for possession of the floor, and ultimately for the status that winning an argument gives them. For these reasons, teachers need to carefully construct classroom activities that support reading and literacy so that they are gender-fair and inclusive. Boys need to feel engaged enough to be motivated to participate, whereas girls need to feel included by both content and approach so that they can participate with feelings of safety and confidence. As the following classroom vignette shows, careful attention to these issues of gender can lead to greater learning successes for both girls and boys.

Enacting Gender in the Classroom

Jeff Zabriske's students defy the usual belief that boys don't like to read. A popular eleventh-grade teacher, Jeff runs a boys-only book club before school that is invariably well attended. Yet it is not just in this elective context that boys read willingly. The same is true for his mainstream classes. A brief glance around Jeff's classroom tells the story. There are vibrant posters everywhere of athletes, bikers, and rock stars promoting reading. There are bookshelves filled with contemporary paperbacks, a basketball hoop with a couple of balls, and lots of student art on the walls. Jeff's classroom encourages the kind of *flow* that Smith and Wilhelm (*Reading*) talk about, an immersion in vibrant human activity.

As a teacher and role model, Jeff performs a masculinity that embraces reading as a cool and desirable thing to do. He frequently starts his class by recalling something he has read the night before, texts that he hopes his students will pick up on their own. Today he is introducing his class to Irwin Shaw's first play, *Bury the Dead*, a social satire about a group of soldiers killed in battle who refuse to be buried. Jeff has chosen this play for a number of reasons (in addition to the fact that it was revived off-Broadway in 2008). First among his reasons is that the text can be acted out, literally turning reading into action. Second, it asks everyone—but especially boys—to imagine what it would mean to die in battle. And finally, it gives his class the opportunity to explore the ways in which we expect soldiers to perform a particular kind of masculinity, even at a time when women are serving in combat.

The play is shocking, at times graphic, but it is effective in getting his students to see gender, first as it was constructed in the 1930s and then in a contemporary context, and to realize how masculinity has held on to many of the same characteristics. Students in the class also have read Thomas Hardy's "The Man He Killed," Wilfred Owen's "Dulce et Decorum Est," and sections of Tim O'Brien's *The Things They Carried*. They ask questions about whether gender roles have been in flux for the past couple of centuries or if any of these texts represent gender as we know it today. The play's antiwar message raises questions and creates some controversy, but it gives students in the class an opportunity to talk about the ways in which military personnel today enact their gender and how women are now expanding their performances of gender well beyond the stereotypes of yesteryear. Girls in the class also question the dramatis personae of the play, which contains women only as typically feminine characters. If the play were set in Iraq today, would it be recast to include female soldiers? All of these questions help to draw the students in, and each helps bridge some gap in the social construction of the students' genders.

The following brief slice of classroom conversation provides a window into the ways in which both male and female students view the reading assignments they have encountered and the ideas that their reading has inspired. Jeff begins by attempting to dislocate the play they have just read from its original historical context.

> **Jeff:** What if this play were set in Iraq today? How would it be different?
>
> **Tommy:** The injuries would be different. People are getting their heads and fingers blown apart, but they survive and their families have to cope with what has happened to them. In the play they only had to face their death.

Sarah:	Why do you always have to focus on the gory parts of war, Tommy? War is bigger than just what happens to people physically.
Tommy:	'Cause war is gory.
Jeff:	Well, what else is different about the war in Iraq?
Janie:	Today women are soldiers, too. They can be killed in combat. There are even some husbands and wives serving together.
Bob:	But are they really on the front line in combat? How much has really changed?
Janie:	A lot has! The role of women is completely different now than it was in other wars.
Sara:	But one thing stays the same. War is stupid.
Tommy:	Yeah, it sucks. Why does it keep happening?
Jared:	It keeps happening because there are people like Osama bin Laden. They don't care about what we think is stupid or not stupid. They attack us. They attack innocent people to get what they want. You can't just let them do that. Sometimes you have to go to war.
Jeff:	Those are both good points. We've read literature from two centuries and four wars. Do people have different ideas today about when or why they should go to war, about when wars are justified and when they are not? And what should the role of women be in war? Should they be on the front lines? How do we start to answer these questions?

In this discussion, gender is front and center, as are the presuppositions of many of the students. In some cases, their opinions vary perhaps because of gender, whereas in other cases there is evidence of gender stereotypes being deconstructed. In several cases, though, it seems that participants in this discussion are enacting gender roles that they have learned and accepted as part of their socialization into the cultures in which they were brought up.

Smith and Wilhelm argue that part of the gender gap in literacy achievement is due to "hegemonic masculinities": that is, definitions of masculinity that constrain what young men see as acceptable masculine behavior (*Boys* 363). Martino claims that the activity of reading has become feminized, so boys, in the throes of their gender identity formation, resist the notion that they can both read and perform appropriate masculinities. But what teachers everywhere recognize is this:

in general, adolescent boys and girls do read differently, and to teach them well, we literature teachers need to be able to understand those differences.

Reading and Doing: Gendered Perspectives on the Activity of Reading

Gender is one among several complicating factors that teachers of reading must address in the literature classroom. It serves as a lens for readers, whose views of literature are perhaps inherently colored by their own gender socialization. Long before any of us makes choices about the ways in which we see the world, this powerful social construction tells us what we are *intended* to see, how we are *supposed* to react to what we see, and how these reactions shape the meaning of what we observe. Gender is everywhere, and relatively few people even recognize it as something that can be embraced or resisted. It is simply an omnipresent fact of our lives.

It is not surprising, then, that we should read in concert with a set of gendered presuppositions about who we are as readers, about the ways in which texts reflect us or ignore us, about the importance that texts assign or deny us, and about the ideas that texts make available to us. The identities that literature presents to us—those of characters, of authors, and even of ourselves—are the products of shifting but powerful social forces. The ubiquity of gender makes even conscious resistance of its influence a difficult task. When we think of reading as an activity, then, we see how gender colors our practice of it.

In her book *Gender Trouble: Feminism and the Subversion of Identity*, literary theorist Judith Butler has made a convincing case that gender is not an essential part of human identity. Rather, it is performative; something we enact. It is not what we *are* but what we *do* that constitutes our gender. Many boys act out what they feel, square off against each other in competition, learn to control their pain, talk each other out of negative feelings, and role-play the status they wish to attain. They balk at sitting still, collaborate only with some prodding, and look for opportunities to one-up each other, whereas girls enjoy working together. Many girls, on the other hand, are more reluctant to assert themselves in ways that might be seen as aggressive. When girls perform gender, they defer to boys, display what some call "learned helplessness," assent to standards of fashion and body image while calling attention to those who don't conform, and resist actions that set them apart from their peers. This performance of gender also takes place within a larger context: the vast network of social interactions that recognize gender and prescribe appropriate responses to it. As a socially defined activity, then, reading is a site for the performance of gender, and so we should expect the act of reading to follow gendered patterns.

These gendered patterns are powerful shaping forces in the processes of meaning-making that we are helping our students to explore. In the same way that our identities are shaped by the manners in which social norms dispose us to act, our interpretations of literature are shaped by a series of gender-bound imperatives about action, about values, and about identity. These gender-bound imperatives affect how girls and boys read and interpret literature.

In "*Reading Don't Fix No Chevys*," Smith and Wilhelm articulate a number of general research findings about gender and reading:

- Girls comprehend fiction better than boys.
- Boys seem to prefer nonfiction, magazines, and newspapers.
- Boys tend to prefer short texts or texts with short sections.
- Girls enjoy leisure reading more than boys.
- Many boys enjoy reading about sports and hobbies.
- Some boys enjoy fantasy and science fiction.
- Graphic novels and comic books are more popular with boys than girls.
- Boys prefer visual texts.
- Boys really do judge a book by its cover.

In addition to gendered preferences, we should also expect that the practices of meaning-making will differ for boys and for girls. For example, one teacher confides that whenever she teaches William Faulkner's classic short story "A Rose for Emily," the boys tend to focus on the necrophilia in the story, whereas the girls focus on the tragedy of the romance. Boys often read for plot, even in poetry, whereas girls go symbol hunting (Appleman, *Reading*). We must account for those social practices that are deemed meaningful for each gender. And finally, we must create conditions in our literature classrooms that allow us to interrupt rather than perpetuate gendered patterns of meaning instead of potentially falling victim to these patterns and thus allowing our students to be similarly victimized.

Gender and Language Rituals

If we consider how different boys and girls are from each other in all other aspects of their adolescent lives, we shouldn't be surprised at the differences they exhibit in response to reading. For boys, a best friend is someone you do things with, and doing things is key. Even when they are alone, as Smith and Wilhelm point out, boys want to enjoy the experience of what they do: what Mihaly Csikszentmihalyi described as "flow experiences" involving complete absorption in the activity at hand. Most studies on boys and reading, however, suggest that, for boys, reading is not doing. It doesn't absorb them; they don't lose themselves in it.

The possibility of becoming absorbed in an activity is central to the enjoyment we take from it. In their study of boys and reading, Smith and Wilhelm looked closely at the importance of immediate experience. The boys they interviewed reported that they participate in a variety of activities—from basketball to music to video games—for the joy of the activity. And while the boys in their study acknowledged the instrumental value of reading, their interactions with school-sponsored literature did not produce a "focus on the moment," an immediate experience in which they could lose themselves (*Reading* 41). Reading seemed to these boys to be something quite the opposite: an enforced passivity, lacking both absorption and activity. Unlike writing, as Bruce Pirie said, for boys reading doesn't create tangible products and doesn't hold promise for future accomplishment: "Writing is something you do; it's an activity, it's productive, it influences others to see things your way, and it can make you rich and famous. Reading on the other hand, seems passive and lonely. You go off by yourself and just sit there" (76).

If the boys in Smith and Wilhelm's study are typical, one can imagine further ramifications of gender for in-school reading. Some scholars, like Kindlon, Thompson, and Barker, suggest that typical boys' behavior is actually being pathologized. They see it this way: "In our experience it is evident that most of what is being called ADD today would not have been called ADD fifteen or twenty years ago and that much of it falls within the range of normal boy behavior" (44). Sitting and reading is antithetical to the normal active and exploratory behaviors that provide flow experiences for boys. There should be little surprise, then, that many boys find reading to be tedious rather than exciting.

For Smith and Wilhelm, the performance of gender and school-sponsored reading can be profitably paired if teachers offer a choice of texts, often around a common question. Literature classrooms can flow for boys if the act of reading is part of a larger inquiry about things that matter. And what matters to adolescent boys is not the common textbook themes around which literature anthologies are constructed. Rather, what matters are vital questions like: "How are we implicated in injustice and what can we do about it?" or "How can we better prepare for a disaster?" (Wilhelm and Smith, *Boys* 235).

The Performance of Masculinities and Feminisms

The important and often-cited work of Wayne Martino suggests that boys see reading as unmasculine. He notes that the hypermasculinity often associated with African American males is highly present as well in middle-class white boys, and not just in the United States. Martino's original research was done in Australia, and it has been verified in the United Kingdom and Canada as well. What this research demonstrates is that boys who like reading are frequently labeled by their peers as "faggots" or "gay."

The general idea in Martino's work is that boys police masculinities among themselves. They both seek and enforce enactment of masculinity as a means for achieving desirable heterosexual identities. To do so, they need to think and act in concert with their gender models, and the result is a form of extreme masculinity. As part of this policing structure, they label undesirable behaviors as homosexual, using a variety of pejorative terms against others as a means of enforcement. School curricula that emphasize undesirable behaviors for boys thus find themselves in direct opposition to the prevailing social norms for gender.

Smith and Wilhelm, while they do not contradict Martino, found that the boys in their study did not subscribe to this manner of hypermasculinity (*Reading*). Their study found no inherent opposition between reading and appropriate enactments of gender. While the boys in their study did report a resistance to reading, it was not based on a perception that reading was a feminized activity. Instead, their boys consistently applauded the reading that other boys did. They saw reading as having an instrumental purpose: it would help them in the future to do well in school and to get better jobs. This future focus, though, lacks the necessary immediacy of experience that provides *flow*.

At the same time, they supported reading among those boys who liked it, even praising the activity among their friends. As one of them said, "I don't read that much, but if somebody reads and they really get into it and it's the one thing they really like, I respect 'em for it because that's their thing, they like to read" (Smith and Wilhelm, *Reading* 72). These observations seem to reflect an awareness among young men that education is to be valued for the opportunities it presents for the future, and it includes reading as a part of that future value. This awareness, however, is not sufficient to change the ways in which boys view reading as a part of gender performance. In some way, then, it seems that schools must find ways in which boys can perform reading within the boundaries of conventional gender roles.

Addressing Gender in the Literature Classroom

The good news about gender and reading is that many of our peers have developed successful methods for adapting literature instruction for each gender. In addition to the gender-fair techniques we've already shared, some specific strategies have been successful in engaging boys in reading. The following are some general tips to encourage boys to read.

What Literature Teachers Can Do to Encourage Boys to Read

- Provide choice in reading. Choice is an extremely important aspect in boys' motivation. Choice also seems to increase a sense of ownership and engagement with all readers.

- Make certain to include plenty of nonfiction in your choices. Many boys prefer nonfiction to more traditional literary texts.

- When you do select a text, consider texts that resonate with boys' personal experiences.

- Offer short texts, even magazines, to get things started.

- Make reading social by providing a lot of opportunity for boys to discuss what they've read.

- Provide tons of overt positive encouragement.

- Find and promote male readers as role models. Reading needs to be "cool," something that is part of what it means to be masculine. For example, have male high school students give book talks to middle school students. Or, when possible, invite local authors, both male and female, to visit literature classes.

- Use active learning. Add physical activity and extension activities to the reading curriculum and to reading time (boys' brains learn better with music, movement, etc.).

- Reduce the amount of class time devoted to silent reading. While it may be profitable to use silent reading time for individual conferencing, the lack of activity during silent reading can make class time seem to drag. If you do offer individual reading time, providing students with reading logs, journal assignments, or during-reading activities can make the reading time more active. You also could incorporate some of the strategies we suggested for active reading in Chapter 5, including think-alouds.

- Make narrative retelling an important part of the class. Reading then becomes another way to share stories.

Reading among Girls

Research on gender and language suggests that, in contrast to boys, talk constitutes its own activity among girls. Sharing language is what makes girls best friends. For them, language *is* activity. Talking is doing. Talk creates connection. Conversation is what girls do to enact closeness (Tannen). Given this set of behaviors, it is easy to see why girls are more easily drawn to reading than boys are. They can imagine reading as direct linguistic interaction because their socialization toward language allows them to transform books into silent friends, especially if the book has familiar feminine themes and female characters, or if it in some other way mirrors the things that girls are attracted to in talk. They can sit face-to-face with the narrator and create an emotional bond as they respond to the story.

Among typically socialized girls, conversation has the potential to provide *flow*. The goal is closeness with the other conversant. Their field of attention is often limited to the conversation, and attention and activity can merge as they converse. The rules of conversation dictate that there is immediate feedback in the form of response, an emphasis on sharing that provides an immediate reward, and control of the interaction. While reading and conversation are quite different on several levels, they still share significant characteristics. Language still constitutes a basis of activity, what Louise Rosenblatt called a *transaction*, and this transaction provides opportunity for absorption. Better readers actively predict the direction of a story, for example, and the story then responds, sometimes in concert with a prediction and sometimes in an unexpected direction. For girls, a story *flows*.

Consider, for instance, Esperanza, the narrator of *The House on Mango Street*, which we offered in Chapter 5 as a possible text for struggling readers. The narrator talks to the reader, tells a story, creates a world into which the reader is invited. For many girls, sitting face-to-face with a book is physically like sitting opposite another person. This physical orientation resembles the attitude of conversation among girls. By contrast, when boys are asked to simply sit and talk, they are often immediately uncomfortable. This sort of situation is too passive to be sustained. Boys want to talk about what they're doing, and so they need to be doing something in order to talk. Further, the idea of squaring up to another linguistic source—whether a person or a book—is also clearly uncomfortable. When directed to talk to each other, for example, boys in Deborah Tannen's experiments physically oriented themselves at angles or even sat side-by-side. These findings are important for teachers to consider as we structure discussion both in large- and small-group situations.

In large-group situations, for example, it's best not to rely exclusively on volunteers. Keep track of who talks and when, and orchestrate class discussions more intentionally. It's useful to ask all students to jot down their ideas before they raise their hands or volunteer. Then, since all students should at least theoretically be prepared to speak, the teacher can call on students, striving for gender balance in the classroom discourse.

I've also often used gender-exclusive small groups in my literature classroom, especially when talking about sensitive coming-of-age issues or even of gender itself. Gender-exclusive groups can be more comfortable for a variety of reasons. I then make the "jigsaw move" and reconstruct the groups to include both boys and girls and have them report on what they discussed in class. Another strategy is to assign a group reporter when using small groups rather than have the social landscape of peers dictate who might dominate the discourse. Of course, all of these strategies are useful for any teacher. But they can be particularly helpful in attending to gender patterns in classroom discourse.

If Dead White Men Populate the Canon, Then Why Is It Girls Who Like to Read?

It is likely that the canon itself contributes to the ways in which both boys and girls respond to reading in the literature classroom. The kinds of stories that boys are drawn to—books like those in Gary Paulsen's Hatchet series, for example—often reside outside the canon. Also, the unfamiliar vocabulary of canonical works disturbs the flow of reading when it does occur, producing for many uncertainty, anxiety, and unwanted interruptions in the reading process. To the extent that canonical literature holds sway in classrooms, we can expect that many boys will continue to resist reading. And when they resist reading, they become the struggling readers that we described in Chapter 5.

A key theme among struggling readers is lack of self-efficacy. The less successful readers believe themselves to be, the more tedious and lonely the experience of reading will seem. Thus teachers of reading and literature need to ensure success by matching readers to texts they can decode, comprehend, and interpret. Overmatching—that is, the presentation to students of texts that exceed their reading levels—can occur easily and frequently within a curriculum that stresses cultural literacy or canonical literature, for example. Of course we want our students to be familiar with great works of literature, but teachers must ensure that their students are ready for these encounters, that these encounters are pleasant and fulfilling, and that they are built upon a solid foundation of reading skills that will enable the students to achieve the reading goals that the curriculum prescribes.

The accomplishment of these goals is perhaps easier for girls, who are oriented differently to the experience of reading. Girls are able to have successful encounters with, say, the Bronte sisters because the female characters in these novels enact roles that girls find to be familiar and intriguing yet unassuming and domestic. James Marshall explains it this way:

> The [sentimental] novels showed women characters "saving" the men and children around them through their innate goodness and sacrifice—doing, in other words, precisely what the culture had asked women in general to do.
>
> But though their spiritual goals were lofty, women authors did not claim for themselves the status of high art. In fact, they studiously cultivated an image of their craft as itself domestic, a kind of verbal needle-work, if you will, that found a way to be useful without pomposity or grandeur. (5)

This ability among girls to successfully encounter the dense domestic narratives of the nineteenth century, for example, underscores a crucial difference between the socialization of the sexes. There are, in fact, two levels of challenge that need to be matched in the selection of reading texts: the first is matching of reading ability, while the second is a matching of social expectation. Both boys and girls need to have well-scaffolded reading skills to encounter canonical texts. Girls, however, typically possess greater social practices for reacting to language in ways that create the connection necessary for active imaginative entry into the world of a literary text.

One reasonable conclusion about the selection and presentation of literary texts, then, is that it must be for two levels of readiness: scholastic readiness and social readiness. The first we seem to account for well; the second we too frequently miss or ignore. If we keep in mind the ways in which our students enact gender in their daily activities, and we use this information to determine present readiness, we will ultimately be more successful in constructing their future readiness.

There is a flip side to this story, though, as Barbara Guzzetti points out. Girls often feel marginalized in classrooms, and so their out-of-class appetite for reading may be left at the schoolroom door. The problem is a seeming disenfranchisement in literacy instruction. Too often, Guzzetti found, boys tend to dominate class discussions, even in areas like language arts where girls tend to do very well, and this appears to be the case despite the biological sex of the teacher. Guzzetti's findings are supported by Tannen's research years earlier that suggests that boys are more prone to choose the topics of discussion, hold the floor longer, and interrupt or overlap other speakers. A predisposition toward reading, then, is not enough to ensure success.

Paths to Success

For boys, there appear to be two prerequisites for successful school-sponsored reading. The first is an affective attachment to the reading content itself, and the second is the creation of activities around reading that allow for a desirable enactment of masculinity. Readings for less experienced and more resistant boys should build on their conceptions of masculinity—possibly expanding their understanding of appropriate masculinities—so that reading and gender enactment don't conflict. At the same time, socially active modes of interpretation can relieve boys of the feeling that reading is passive and lonely. Reading, then, needs to constitute an action in itself, and it needs to lead to action in the interpretive process.

There is some good news to be found in the expansion of the literary canon. If one purpose of literature is to represent the experiences of a broader range of people and cultures, then granting the status of literature to a greater number of literary works can translate into a greater variety of experiences to be offered by the canon. This variety can then open up new literary reading experiences to members of both genders, but especially to boys. A greater range of personal and social experiences become salient to the interpretation of literary texts, and a greater variety of activities can be represented in ways that allow younger and less able readers to become absorbed in the processes of reading.

One central question we should ask to create the conditions for success is this: how do the contents of the texts we teach match with the gender socialization of the students who will read them? Before we can think about revealing gender normative behavior or subverting gender stereotypes, we must clearly understand the ways in which our students' lives have been shaped by these norms. If our teaching practices do not allow readers to reflect upon their own socially meaningful experiences, then we have little hope that they will construct meanings for the texts they encounter.

Consider, for example, the desire boys have to experience ideas actively. Even if literature enables only vicarious experience of action, there must nonetheless be action present. By maximizing the element of action, then, we might have a better chance of inspiring boys to acts of meaning-making. Bruce Pirie suggests, for example, a greater emphasis on drama in high school English since it is inherently active. It builds around action, and it can be acted out. By extension, this concept of *acting out* is going to be gendered in accordance with social construction.

Conclusion

In light of these studies, it appears to be the case that behaviors of reading mirror behaviors in most other areas of our larger societies. To the extent that gender influences our performances of masculinities and feminine social norms, so will reading be influenced. If these stereotypical performances are allowed to continue unmitigated, it is likely that both sides will suffer. The notion of a post-gender classroom may still be decades away. However, if literature teachers understand the gender issues inherent in every classroom, they can begin to disrupt and trouble these traditional patterns. Perhaps they might even be able to exploit them to help students understand and challenge the social norms that literary narratives so frequently portray.

That social norms reproduce themselves in literature is not surprising, but we may be surprised at how our students understand the messages that narratives deliver. Kate Chopin's *The Awakening*, for example, is frequently viewed as a feminist text, but even girls can dismiss the potential power of the text by saying, "That's what you get for rejecting your family. You end up alone and dead by suicide. The message is that we should not be like Edna." Their gender socialization will not yet allow them to ask whether Edna was a woman loved and missed by her family or swallowed whole by her family. Gender socialization is a powerful cognitive predisposition, even before it is enacted. We should heed the example of Jeff Zabriske, then, who exposes gender's machinery as he teaches literature.

In addition to the kinds of approaches that Jeff offers, we can invite students to consider the social construction of gender by introducing them to feminist or gender theory as we read literary texts. Whether it is a traditional "feminist" text such as *The Awakening*, or traditional texts in which feminist theory can refresh and reimagine the female characters of Hemingway, Faulkner, Steinbeck, and Fitzgerald, among others, or a work of contemporary fiction, the feminist lens can help students rethink the role of gender in the world of texts and in their world as well.

These techniques will enhance the engagement of reading for both boys and girls. It may also help address some of the differences in literacy achievement between the genders that have been documented by a variety of assessments. And it is the ubiquity of assessment, for better or worse, that we take up in the next chapter. It is time to reclaim the assessment of reading, on our own terms, in the literature classroom.

Chapter Seven

Reading Assessment in the Literature Classroom: Reclaiming the Agenda

It comes as no surprise to education professionals that standardized assessment drives the public's perception of school achievement, and this includes what we think we know about how students are reading. Most of us know, too, that the right assessment tools are invaluable to good teaching practice. They help us understand what our students know, how they learn it, where gaps in their learning might lie, and how much they can learn in any given period. These measures, however, are not provided by standardized assessments. And so classroom teachers need a rich array of assessment tools to offer alternatives to the single-point measure of standardized tests. If we are going to responsibly address the immediate needs of our students, it is important that we offer our students *formative assessment* throughout their literature instruction that can serve as a counterpoint to the skill-and-drill mentality that too often arises from these standardized assessments.

Formative assessment allows teachers to check on the progress of student learning while that learning is taking place. This evaluation of learning in progress helps both teachers and students make readjustments to increase learning. For example, in the literature classroom, teachers often give nongraded reading checks to make certain that students comprehend literary texts as they read. It makes little pedagogical sense to wait until they've finished the novel to find out that they are having difficulty understanding it. Literature teachers also provide formative assessments of the variety of academic concepts and apparatus surrounding literary interpretation. To enhance literary understanding, literature teachers revisit literary terms and critical theories throughout the reading experience. Classroom teachers also use many of the cognitive reading strategies we've discussed in previous chapters to help students keep track of their sense-making as they read. These strategies—predicting, summarizing, think-alouds, reflecting and refining meaning, and evaluating, among others—are really formative assessments that students employ as they read and that teachers can use to stay on top of student learning. In addition, literature teachers can provide ongoing formative assessments of student writing; they focus on writing papers as a process with discrete steps so that students can receive constructive feedback before the final paper is due. Many teachers often read penultimate drafts before providing a final assessment, another example of formative rather than summative assessment. These kinds of small-scale assessments hold great sway in the lived classroom experiences of students and teachers, but these are not the kinds of assessments that interest policymakers.

The fact of the matter is that large-scale standardized testing is important to policymakers. It helps them locate so-called achievement gaps and perhaps measure the effectiveness of state- or district-wide policy decisions. At the same time, though, there is little if anything that a typical classroom teacher can do with a standardized assessment score. That number doesn't tell us which individual students need help most, nor does it direct our teaching practice to address that student's needs. Toward those ends, in this chapter, I will review a number of possible in-class, formative, and targeted approaches to assessment and provide examples of formative assessments that can be easily incorporated into a teacher's regular literature curriculum. First, though, we need to review some of the problems raised by standardized assessments for reading and literature classrooms.

First, there is the issue of students reading "below grade level." While this is a problem that the public can easily understand, it is hardly as clear-cut as a reading-level score might suggest. Grade-level reading scores are averages, and so it is a numerical impossibility that all students will read at grade level. Thus, while reading-level scores for individual students may be an indicator of need for individual students, they serve as little more. Once those scores are in, it is up to the classroom teacher to interpret what the scores might indicate (if anything) and decide what will happen next.

Another problem with standardized reading assessments involves the different aptitudes and interests of students as reading needs shift. For instance, as we've discussed in this book, students are not equally adept at reading in all genres. Those who read narratives well will perhaps exceed expectations in reading history as well as fiction, but they may not interpret analytical texts with the same degree of proficiency. Students who are deeply motivated by interactive texts—hypertext, social networking, text messaging, etc.—may find themselves disengaged by linear and noninteractive texts. Reading that requires scaffolded knowledge as well as scaffolded reading skills will cause difficulties for those students who lack background information and thus complicate any conclusions we can draw from typical large-scale assessments.

Yet another problem associated with standardized assessments involves a lack of affective connection to the reading materials of a given reading requirement. This emotional link to reading provides intrinsic motivation to those who find it while leaving the rest to varying degrees of boredom and inactivity. It seems that all of us today, not just young people, have come to expect a broad range of resources that will appeal to our personal interests. The postmodern newsstand dwarfs its modern predecessor. Cable and satellite television and radio provide literally hundreds of simultaneous viewing and listening options. The Internet seems to provide access to nearly everything. At the same time, though, standardized assessments ensure that the reach of formal education will remain narrow. Educational legislation, it seems, has been successful in beating back postmodern education with a big stick. Still, somehow teachers must address the range of student abilities and interests if they are going to accomplish the goals they have for their students' literacy. As we have seen throughout this book, the needs, interests, and abilities of students in the literature classroom vary considerably. Teachers need to assess how factors such as gender, learning context, prior school experiences, and the socially mediated context of learning contribute to a student's literacy learning or struggle. Unfortunately, large-scale assessment, popular though it may be with policymakers, does not provide teachers with the specific information they need to create literacy instruction for all their students.

Local and formative assessments, on the other hand, allow teachers to say exactly how and where their students are succeeding. They also allow teachers and schools to identify the additional resources they need. By using a range of classroom assessment techniques, then, teachers can better serve the immediate needs of their students.

Accounting for Students' Performance

Despite the problems associated with standardized reading tests, virtually every public school teacher today is required to account for student performance according to one set of measures or another. There are national standardized tests, state-mandated exams, district- and schoolwide scope and sequence plans, and departmental vertical planning documents to be considered when building curriculum. The reality is that all of these mandates contribute to an individual teacher's classroom assessment decisions. First, they offer a range of achievement targets and learning criteria. Second, they reflect the standards of the communities in which we teach. Third, they provide programmatic coherence for our shared instructional goals. The first step for teachers in setting up useful classroom assessments, then, is to review and prioritize the criteria and objectives set forward for the students through these mandates.

A natural starting point would be for teachers to identify common criteria: the expectations for one's classrooms and students that are clearly articulated across the spectrum of testing sites. For example, the National Assessment of Educational Progress defines both *reading contexts* and *aspects of reading* within its summary of criteria. For literature teachers, the following description of *reading contexts* offers a series of very general points of focus upon which students are tested at the fourth- and eighth-grade levels: "Reading for literary experience includes exploring events, characters, themes, settings, plots, actions, and the language of literary works by reading novels, short stories, poems, plays, legends, biographies, myths, and folktales" (U.S. Department of Education 4). Teachers can match these expectations for literary reading with their state and local criteria and then build classroom objectives around a continuing focus on those expectations that are most frequently noted. In schools where students already meet these objectives or excel in particular reading contexts, teachers may choose to develop more challenging objectives.

As to the NAEP's *aspects of reading*, these expectations reflect the degree to which they believe knowledge schemas should be developed by the fourth and eighth grades. Since knowledge schemas serve such an important role in the reading achievement of individual students, the NAEP's *aspects of reading* might also serve as a basis for addressing specific knowledge sets required for successful reading. In terms of how these aspects connect to issues we've raised in this book, teachers may want to emphasize the general understanding and interpretation of texts, a connection between the reader and the text, and explicit knowledge of both the content and the structure of the text itself.

What Students Need to Be Successful

Before discussing specific assessment strategies or instruments, we should also review the general knowledge and skills that contribute most to successful reading. While it would be good if we could arrange these knowledge and skill sets hierarchically, we must also acknowledge that—despite what state curricula often tell us—students do not build these knowledge bases sequentially or discretely, nor do they build them in a single instructional unit or year. Still, there are scaffolding principles that determine more immediate and less immediate points of attention in reading instruction, spanning what we might consider instruction in *reading* to instruction in *literature*. These can be outlined around a variety of learning schemas.

First, students need to build on their innately acquired linguistic knowledge. While this provides a basis for grammatical understanding, every language has its own lexicon, and within this lexicon there resides a variety of individual facts: what each word sounds like, the extent of the word's meanings, the syntactic frame into which the word fits, the social values associated with that word, and so on. Students must also become familiar with the complex array of English verb tenses, active and passive voice, and what classical grammarians would have called *mood* (indicative, subjunctive) before they can be certain of what happened and when within any complex written text. Likewise, they need to recognize and understand the nature of syntactic transformations and inversions in order to ascertain sentence-level meaning.

A similar, almost parallel, set of knowledge bases comes into play when we read literature: what the genre of the work is and what we expect from each genre; the concepts (social, cultural, historical, personal, ethnic, psychological, or political) with which readers of the work must be familiar; the conventions associated with national, historical, and political literatures; and the extent of specific linguistic knowledge required for the successful interpretation of that text (diction, syntax, arrangement, point of view, etc.).

To account for students' prior and present achievement in building these bases of knowledge, teachers must make specific decisions about what they need to assess in their classrooms and how they will assess it accurately. As a starting point, then, teachers may want to assess—sometimes formally and sometimes informally—these general markers of successful reading:

- Prior reading experiences
- Vocabulary and word identification skills
- Ability to recognize word meaning in context
- Reading comprehension skills
- Oral language skills
- Subject-matter knowledge
- The reader's self-efficacy
- Textual analysis skills
- Knowledge application skills (of texts to "real-world" situations)
- Meaning negotiation

Not everything on this list of reading skills requisites needs to be addressed at every level or in every class, but this list demonstrates the range of items that teachers can assess to make the best determinations about their students' learning needs.

Toward this end, we can distinguish a variety of possible assessment strategies for everyday classroom use. For example, you can have students answer one or two quick questions about specific elements of the text (plot, characterization, structure) on half-sheets of paper and discuss them in class. You can question students orally and take note of their clarity of understanding or points of confusion. You can have students fill out KWL charts or other graphic organizers and use them to assess their knowledge of the textual worlds they inhabit as they are in them. I like to pass out index cards at least twice a week and ask students the following questions:

- What's one thing you heard today in class that was interesting?
- What's one thing we did today that you found confusing?
- What's one thing in the reading you did for today that you'd like to learn more about?
- What's one question you have for me?

Questions and Concerns for Assessing Literary Reading

As part of a scaffolded reading program, assessment of each of the following concerns will aid teachers and their departments in making determinations about aspects of their curriculum. The list of possible assessment items and techniques that follows is not strictly sequential, but it is roughly prioritized to follow good practices in the teaching of reading within the framework of a literature classroom. A brief review of each concern is included to make the selection and integration of these techniques clearer.

Assessing Prior Reading Experience

Because both knowledge and skills are built in context, a logical starting point for assessment of student achievement in literary reading is a review of past reading experiences. The object of this assessment is to discover not just what students have read (since this can often be discovered by other means), but what they have taken away from those experiences. Our hope is that they will remember the subject of the work, the genre into which it fits, the conventions of that genre, and something of their transactions with that text as they worked to interpret it. We can later revisit the texts they have read to see what was included by way of vocabulary, syntax, conceptual information, and thematic content. A list of possible questions and prompts for assessing prior reading experience might include the following.

About You and Your Reading Life

Name _____

1. What literary texts that you have read do you find most memorable? Or what do you remember from your reading of _____. (A specific text that you know the student has read.) [This question assesses reading comprehension.]

2. What do you remember about this text, and what did you like most about it? [This item addresses students' thematic and affective responses.]

3. How would you describe the kind of text this is? [This is a test of genre knowledge.]

The answers elicited by these questions should reveal several things about student reading experiences. First, they will tell us what students remember about their reading of a particular text (and they may divulge some information about the extent to which students are actually reading assigned texts as opposed to simply learning information about those texts). The second item provides information about students' affective responses to texts and could give clues as to the types of activities that will improve their emotional engagement with new literary experiences. Third, because genre knowledge is tied directly to readers' expectations about a text, a review of generic features of various texts will help students anticipate what it is they are intended to learn from a given reading experience.

Vocabulary and Word Identification Skills

One of the keys to successful reading at any level is vocabulary knowledge. Again, this entails not just definitions of words, but knowledge of their use in context: the ways in which specific lexical items actually dictate the syntax of the sentences that contain them. Readers need to recognize words in context, know their definitions in context, and understand the concepts that those words represent. To test pronunciation, this assessment would be given orally.

- Pronounce and define each of the following words from "Young Good-man Brown," making sure that your definition fits the context and usage of the word in this story: *benignantly, consorting, howbeit, lore, visages, similitude, repute, score.* [Phonemic awareness, word recognition]
- What do these words mean in the context of this story? [Word recognition in context]
- Why might the selection of these words by the author be particularly important? [Concept familiarity]
- How does the selection of these words affect the tone of the story? [Connotation]

There is evidence that word identification serves as a predictor for reading com-prehension, although this predictive quality diminishes as readers get older. Still, the more quickly readers can identify words, the more fluently they will read and the better they will comprehend texts. They also will read more text in any fixed period of time.

When we take into account the fact that, according to the *Oxford English Dictionary*, the English language has an active lexicon of approximately 170,000 words—approximately four times the number of words in the French language—we realize both the richness and the burden that literature in English presents to its readers. More important, though, students from higher socioeconomic status (SES) backgrounds generally are exposed to more written texts and are much more likely to acquire broader bases of both words and concepts in English than students from lower SES backgrounds. Testing for word-level background and ability to recognize words is thus a critical point of assessment for teachers of students from diverse backgrounds.

Conceptual knowledge provides important bases for thinking as well as read-ing skills, and thus to teach reading successfully teachers must ensure that their students are building a solid range of concepts through their experiences in read-ing. Eleanor Rosch has demonstrated that the cognitive categories we construct—which are marked by abstract words—have prototypical associations that both build on and guide the ways in which we think in categories. George Lakoff has argued independently that concepts and the terms that mark them serve as catego-ries for thinking and for organizing the world. It is important that teachers be able to identify conceptual gaps before presenting literary texts whose interpretation requires a familiarity with specific categories and concepts.

Ability to Recognize Word Meaning in Context

The English word-stock and the English spelling system present challenges to even the most experienced readers.

First, for example, there is the problem of homonyms, words that are spelled alike but have different meanings, like *left* (opposite of right) and *left* (past tense of leave) or *bear* (ursine animal) and *bear* (carry). English also contains homophones: words that sound the same but have different spellings and meanings (*no* and *know*). Third, some words change pronunciation in different contexts but do not change spelling, like the present- and past-tense forms of the verb *to read*. English also has words that cross from one grammatical category to another without changing spelling but with a change in syllable stress (for example, the noun *con'-tent* and the verb *con-tent'*). Many words that shift meaning or sound depending on their context. The following questions, then, will help us determine the extent of students' familiarity with words whose sounds and spellings overlap those of other words. This oral assessment, for example, would help assess students' readings of Faulkner's "A Rose for Emily."

---

1. How is this word pronounced in this textual setting? *august, cedar-bemused, Sartoris, tableau,* noblesse oblige, *craned* (silk), *jalousies, tedious* (brushes)
2. What other words does each of these words resemble? [Differentiation of lexical items]
3. What does each word mean in its respective setting?

When we find homonym errors in our students' writing, we can comfortably assume that their matching of oral language skills and written language skills is incomplete, usually because of a lack of experience with the latter. They know how the language sounds, but they don't always know how specific items from the language are written. Each variant spelling and sound, then, offers an opportunity for an incorrect interpretation.

Reading Comprehension and Memory

One simple test of reading comprehension is the ability to remember what we have just read. Our ability to encode in memory details from a written text is evidence of our understanding of those details. Another frequently used structure for testing comprehension is the KWL strategy, which asks students to answer questions about what they Know, what they Want to know, and what they Learned after reading a text. The following questions serve as generic samples for use of the KWL framework. While this KWL framework can be quickly modified to fit nearly any literary work, these questions continue to address Faulkner's short story.

Understanding What You Have Read

1. What do you remember most clearly from your reading of "A Rose for Emily"? What makes this part of the story memorable for you? [Comprehension and memory]

2. What do you know about this literary work? What is it about? What is its story? [Know]

3. What else do you want to know about Emily Grierson and her life? [Want to know]

4. What do you think you have learned as a result of reading this story? What do you now think about or understand differently? [Learn]

Comprehension skills provide an essential basis for meaning negotiation and other later tasks in the students' transactions with literary texts. The previous assessment items provide opportunities to check on critical background knowledge, levels of student interest (which correlates with memory encoding), and patterns of learning. Low scores in comprehension assessment might indicate a possible overmatching of students with specific literary texts, a perception on the students' part that a literary text does not relate closely enough with their personal and cultural experiences, or perhaps insufficient scaffolding for the text selection at hand.

Oral Language Skills

Answers to questions in this type of assessment would be given orally by students, and those students selected to answer these questions might be selected by the teacher randomly or in a targeted sample to discern the range of skills across the class population. Here is a possible assessment built to assess students' success at reading "Jabberwocky."

1. How do you pronounce the following words (presented on the board or in another written form): *gimble, gyre, wabe, frumious, brillig*? [Phonemic awareness]

2. How would you choose to read these lines (presented in written form) in order to best bring out their meaning or the intent of the narrator? [Oral language skills, prosodic reading]

3. In your own words, how would you describe the beamish boy, the Jabberwock, battle that takes place? [Oral language skills, meaning negotiation]

Because our experience with spoken language long predates our experience with written texts, it serves as a foundation for reading. While literacies obviously require skills not acquired through innate language development, they correspond to and make use of the same grammatical rules. A review of students' oral language skills can reveal a variety of crucial information: the degree to which their acquired oral grammars match the grammar of Standard English, the extent of their vocabulary development, and their ability to use elaborated codes. These abilities typically correlate with abilities in literary reading.

Subject–Matter Knowledge

While it is possible to understand the content of a literary work without explicit or specific subject-area knowledge, meaning is more easily available to readers who possess this knowledge. For example, Randall Jarrell's "Death of the Ball Turret Gunner" carries an unmistakable message, but it is much harder to interpret if one has no idea what the ball turret of a B-17 or B-24 bomber was or looked like. Sometimes, then, it is essential to assess a reader's knowledge of the historical, social, or physical circumstances described within a literary text. Here is a sample assessment geared toward Jarrell's poem.

Poetry and the Experiences It Describes

1. When and where is this poem set?

2. How would you describe the gunner? What do you think he was like?

3. What does a ball turret look like? Draw a picture below.

4. What do you think it was like to sit in a ball turret?

This assessment does three things. First, it tests the students' background knowledge: about World War II and bombing raids over Europe, about an airman's experiences in that war, and about the weapons and dangers that soldiers faced. Second, it ensures that students have sufficient knowledge of the poem to visualize the subject of the poem. And third, it assesses the effectiveness of classroom techniques designed to create the students' reading experience, here specifically, a set of personal and affective responses based on empathy with a literary character.

The Reader's Self-Efficacy

One of the most difficult things to assess in the literature classroom is a student's ability to interpret a work of literature. Because interpretation is a skill, we need to assess it differently from a base of knowledge. We can, of course, assess a specific interpretation, often taking into account the pieces of an interpretive act that are built upon our lectures, peer discussion, and secondary source material, but it is difficult to know what will happen in any student's transaction with the next literary text we present. What we can assess, though, is a student's degree of confidence in approaching such a task. Presuming that our feedback to students is both accurate and helpful, we can ask students about their level of confidence in acts of interpretation. While our students' assessment of their own skills may differ from our assessment of them, it is nonetheless important that students feel comfortable and confident in these acts of interpretation. To assess this degree of self-efficacy, we can ask them to evaluate their own levels of confidence in applying specific skills.

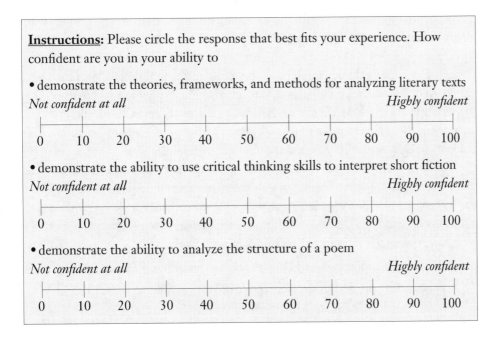

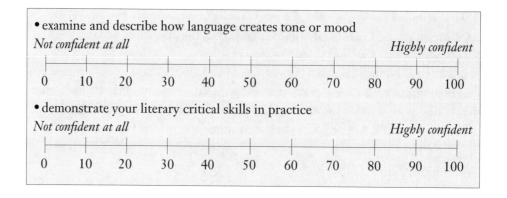

The students' responses to this set of self-confidence questions allow us to focus our instruction on the skills that they report being least certain of. It may well be that they are more able than they believe themselves to be, but by modeling the ways in which these interpretive skills are applied and by giving them additional practice at doing so, we can expect them to perform with greater confidence than they previously had.

Textual Analysis Skills

Both the beauty and the bane of literary texts is that they present their audiences with myriad points of interest and significance. One of the most sophisticated tasks that students undertake in the process of reading, for example, is the determination of salience of items within the text: the ability to distinguish those details that are crucial to interpretation from those that are not. We tell students, for instance, about the intentionality of the author, the idea that everything found in the text was placed there on purpose. The question they face is, "What was the purpose?" Clues for answering this question might be found in the traditional elements upon which literary study has focused, and, not surprisingly, many of these are the elements named in the NAEP's *contexts for reading* in literary texts. In addition to characters, themes, settings, and plots, literary study traditionally has introduced students to elements of language that direct our assignment of meaning: metaphor, metonymy, symbolism, irony, hyperbole, and other schemes and tropes. We make a reasonable assumption when we recognize these tropes that, since they are less common in everyday language than in literature, they must be significant. To assess our students' ability to recognize and interpret such features of literary language, we can ask questions directly about their use:

- Why does Sandburg say, "The fog comes in on little cat feet"?
- What is the source domain (the source of known information) in Emily Dickinson's line, "Hope is the thing with feathers"?

- What does the green light at the end of the pier symbolize for Jay Gatsby?
- Why does Jonathan Swift's narrator advocate that we eat the babies of the poor?
- Why did Walter Dean Myers title his novel *Monster*?

Assessment questions can be written to elicit both information about and practical interpretation of any particular trope or scheme, and the answers to these questions will provide information about the degree to which students can apply their understanding of these forms of literary language.

Knowledge Application Skills (of Text to "Real-World" Situations)

While lovers of literature and of the liberal arts frequently make the argument that literature has value for its own sake, the practical and instrumental focuses of education today often require us to demonstrate the applied value of literary study. More important, though, when our students make connections between literature and the larger world, they in fact demonstrate their skills in literacy. One way to show depth of understanding in a literary text is to make connections between that text and the people and events of the world around us. As some of the model assessment questions next might demonstrate, literature shows its full promise through this kind of application.

- If Jonathan Swift were writing "A Modest Proposal" today, where would it be set and what problem might his ironic argument address?
- How might Shakespeare have made use of images from mass media if he were writing "My mistress' eyes are nothing like the sun" in the twenty-first century?
- What does Robert Frost's "The Road Not Taken" say and not say about the choices available to new high school graduates?
- How do we interpret Ralph Ellison's *Invisible Man* differently after the election of the United States' first African American president?
- What does *Montana 1948* say about the social construction of masculinity?
- Does the novel *Peace Like a River* meet the standards of literary quality that you are used to in your literature classes?
- In what ways do the short stories of Sherman Alexie contribute to our understanding of the situation of Native peoples in contemporary America?

These questions ask at least three things of the students who would answer them. First, they ask for interpretive information about the work in question. Second, they ask the student to locate that information in a specific historical, cultural, or political context. Third, they ask students to make relevant comparisons in order to demonstrate their understanding of a literary text outside of its original context.

Teachers who can get their students to answer these questions well will demonstrate the best principles of literary instruction.

Meaning Negotiation

In the terms laid out by Louise Rosenblatt, literary reading is *transaction*: literally, the text acting upon the reader and the reader acting upon the text. At the conclusion of this transaction there should be an agreement between what the text makes available and what the reader deems meaningful. Possible meaning becomes actual meaning through a process of negotiation, an alignment of experience and understanding. To assess students' ability to negotiate with such texts, we can consider a few model questions about famously ambiguous poems:

- What possible portraits of the father can you construct from the text of Theodore Roethke's "My Papa's Waltz," and which to you seems most plausible?
- At the conclusion of "The Road Not Taken," when Robert Frost says, "And that has made all the difference," what reasons do you have to think that the difference is positive?
- In Judith Ortiz Cofer's "Latin Women Pray," explain why you think that the women's prayers are heard or not heard.

Each of these questions is open-ended, and as such each not only admits multiple answers but also requires the students to draw interpretive conclusions about the text. The ability of students to answer these questions credibly gives assurance that they are able to negotiate meaning in literary texts. An inability to do so would signal a need to return to the text for further reading and review.

Conclusion

To ensure that students are reading literature successfully, teachers need to focus on student performance in their own classrooms, and they need to be free to do so. While national, state, and district imperatives all shape the curricula of literary study, teaching practice must be tailored, school by school, classroom by classroom, and student by student. Depending on the immediate learning objectives of the day, in-class assessment will take a variety of shapes, address learning at different levels, and quite possibly indicate a range of different teaching strategies in otherwise comparable classrooms.

The keys to success, of course, include well-scaffolded reading assignments, appropriate levels of challenge for each group of students, and support for the specific tasks that students are asked to carry out. Teaching to a standard curriculum, on the other hand, potentially denies teachers the ability to address the specific needs of their students. Should this be the case, classroom assessment presents direct evidence of student needs and a justification for curricular variances. It may also indicate a need for changes to the larger curriculum that will accommodate actual levels of student performance.

If our assessments reflect our curricular goals, our classrooms will be places of learning with clarity and purpose. That coherence will go a long way to providing students with pleasurable reading experiences, so that their literacy engagement with texts of all kinds will continue long after they've left our classroom. It is precisely that extension of literacy activity that we take up in the next chapter.

Chapter Eight

Reaching Outward: From Adolescent to Adult Literacy

T his book began with a story from the year I spent teaching literature to incarcerated men; it's a cautionary tale about how high the
stakes are if we fail our students in offering them the literacy skills
that really are their civil rights (Greene). While such dire consequences of inadequate literacy instruction are sobering, there is another, more
heartening side to the literacy story of my incarcerated students. Although the
results of the reading survey that I discussed in Chapter 1 revealed some dis-
connect between their own reading interests and the school-sponsored reading
activities they were provided, many of these men have become avid readers
as adults. Twenty out of the thirty people I surveyed reported reading at least
twenty books a year (Appleman and Schmit). Here are some of their responses
to the survey question, "How do you feel about reading?"

- Reading is an art that should be appreciated. Reading things can allow you to make your own interpretation of what you've read. To me it's a form of meditation.
- Reading is a great tool for learning.
- Very enjoyable if you read material you are interested in. Everyone should be able to read.
- It's the most important recreational tool that I have.
- Reading and learning is food for the soul.
- I believe reading in a sense leads to great wisdom.
- It opens doors to other worlds or cultures.

For these men, reading is no longer an arcane and irrelevant school-sponsored subject; it's an essential life skill. Somehow, in the developmental arc of adolescent readers, we need to situate reading outside of our classroom ways so that it becomes woven deeply into the fabric of our students' adult literacy lives, long after they've left our literature classrooms. Consider the following scene, a sharp contrast, to be sure, to my prison classroom, but one that shares the same goal of fostering adult literacy.

In a small community library of a midwestern city on a sleepy Saturday morning, an unlikely group of readers has begun to gather. There are seven or eight adults, some in their thirties or forties, some considerably older. There are also about the same number of adolescents, who look to be about fifteen or sixteen. The only thing they all seem to have in common is that they are each clutching a copy of the graphic novel *Persepolis* by Marjane Satrapi. When an English teacher from the local high school invites the group to sit down in a circle, it is clear that they have come in pairs, an adolescent accompanied by a parent, a grandparent, or an older friend or mentor.

After a couple of introductory comments, Sarah, the English teacher, invites the group to begin discussing the novel.

Janie (high school junior):	I really liked this book.
Pat (Janie's mom):	Well, I have to say I've never read anything quite like this before.
Janie:	Me neither, but I really thought it was cool. I loved her style of drawing, so stark in black and white and all.
Andrew (high school junior):	I dunno, Janie, it seemed weird, like reading a comic book or something.

George (Andrew's grandfather):	Well, it's not like any comic book I ever read, that's for sure.
	Laughter
Sarah:	Let's talk a bit, shall we, about the content as well as the format of the book. What did you think?
Jeff (high school sophomore):	It's crazy to think how relevant it is today, with all this crazy stuff going on in Iran and everything.
Rick (Jeff's dad):	Do you actually talk about all that stuff in English class, Jeff?
Jeff:	It depends on the book, I guess.
Pat:	I remember reading *Huck Finn* when I was in your grade.
Janie:	We still do, but like in tenth grade. And if you think about it, *Persepolis* is a story about growing up, too. Same thing. Only different.
	Laughter

This lively, wide-ranging, intergenerational conversation is about an unusual contemporary text, one that raises developmental, literary, and political issues. This is a community book club meeting, sponsored by the high school, to help adolescent and adult literacy practices come together around a common text.

This chapter offers suggestions for extending the community of readers in our classrooms out into the community at large. For young people to be inclined to read into adulthood, reading needs to be seen as an act that adults voluntarily engage in. Because of both the texts we teach and the ways we teach them—burdened, for example, by response apparatus, student-friendly though it may be—reading is often seen as schoolish, adolescent, and feminine. Finally, the chapter considers the ways in which we can encourage adolescents, who frequently read only because of our requirement that they do so, to become adults who read out of their own desire.

The Call of the Book Club

Nothing warms an English teacher's heart like the sight of a crowded bookstore. The often-attached coffee shop can't account for the enthusiastic readers that mill around browsing for titles, both classic and contemporary, that haven't been assigned by any English teacher. In addition to these visible signs that adults of all ages and all walks of life read voluntarily, there are other signs of the vibrancy of adult literacy as well. Many people belong to social networking sites like Goodreads, where people from all over the world share their opinions of books recently read. Here is a description of the book club phenomenon that I wrote a few years back:

> We're a book club-crazy nation. From airport lobbies to morning television shows to coffee klatches in suburban cul-de-sacs, it seems as if more and more people are reading novels and discussing them with their peers. Oprah didn't exactly start the movement, but we must reluctantly admit that she's given book clubs and a lot of good books a powerful Middle American push. Recent surveys have indicated that book buying has never been higher. Novels come with ready-made book club guides, and there is even a recent bestselling novel about a book club, *The Jane Austen Book Club*, by Karen Jay Fowler. The steady crowds at bookstores like Barnes and Noble are enough to bring a smile to even the most cynical English teacher. (*Reading* 1)

Since I wrote those words, book clubs both in and out of classrooms have been increasing in number. Libraries across the country offer a service to their patrons called "book club in a bag." Ten copies of a wide range of titles plus a discussion guide are loaned out for up to six weeks. The following is a typical book-club-in-a-bag blurb.

Book-Club-in-a-Bag!

The Nashville Public Library now provides "Book-Club-in-a-Bag" kits to book groups. This gives you the opportunity to conduct book discussions like those that take place at the library—but with Book-Club-in-a-Bag, you can do it wherever and whenever you like.

We now offer a selection of fifteen book club titles, and the list will grow over time. Each is packaged in an attractive and convenient canvas tote bag. The book bags are available in several genres: Southern fiction, Sci-Fi, Romance, African American fiction, Mysteries, Contemporary Christian fiction—a little something for everyone.

Each bag contains:
- Ten copies of a book
- Discussion questions for the book
- Author biography
- Tips for starting a successful book club

> How to Borrow a Book-Club-in-a-Bag:
> - Bags may be checked out for six weeks. They are not renewable.
> - The kit will be checked out on the library card of the person picking up the bag. That patron is completely responsible for the bag and all of its contents.
> - No more than one kit may be borrowed at one time by a patron.
> - You may place holds on the kits through our catalog.

What all of this adult literacy activity seems to indicate is that reading can become not only a lifetime skill but also a lifetime pleasure. Unfortunately, our classroom practices, which are often grounded in the premise that literature is an enterprise to be studied rather than an art form to be enjoyed, frequently fail to turn adolescent language arts students into enthusiastic adult readers. Too frequently, as Sam Intrator and Robert Kunzman point out, adolescents experience their curricular experiences in our classrooms as "boring, boring, boring" (17).

Adolescents who do find reading to be a boring, difficult, and onerous task when they are students are not likely to become members of book clubs or, more broadly, part of the community of literate adults. To encourage the continuation of reading after our students leave our classrooms, English teachers need to consider how we might be able to present reading as an adult activity while they are in our classrooms.

Developmental Issues for Adult Literacy

First, let's consider some of the developmental issues that undergird our assumptions about the transitions between adolescent and adult literacy, which actually means we may need to reconsider our assumptions about adolescence itself.

As we think about how to construct bridges between adolescent and adult literacy, we need to be mindful that in many ways adolescents are already adults, and that adolescence is in and of itself a kind of social construct. Donna Alvermann, for example, reminds us that that there are various "social and cultural constructions of adolescence" (15) that, for better or worse, inform our conceptions, indeed, our ideological constructions, of what adolescence, as well as adolescent literacy, is. She also reminds us that "adolescence is a contested space filled with contradictory constructions of who adolescents are and what they're about" (19).

Moje, Overby, Tsvaer, and Morris point out that "young people's changing independent status and their advancing cognitive development may play a role in their thinking about the practices of literacy" (110). These developmental factors also play a role in how adolescents respond to the pedagogical practices of our literature classrooms.

Too frequently in our practice we tend to infantilize adolescents through text selection and the accompanying classroom activities, which often seem pointless or artificial. We underestimate our students' life experiences, even their worldliness. Moje and her colleagues point out that others have researched what they call the developmental mismatch between secondary school settings and adolescent needs (110).

Both parents and teachers need to be mindful of the permeable boundary between adolescence and adulthood. The chasm we tend to perceive between them is, as Alvermann and others have pointed out, as much mythology as it is reality. By acknowledging the adult that is already in the adolescent and foreshadowing what adult literacy might mean in our classrooms, we may be better able to help our adolescent students transition into adult literacy practices. Although this may sound difficult, there are several concrete factors English teachers can consider as we move our principles into practice.

The Element of Choice

Choosing texts is an important element in fostering adult literacy practices. After all, part of being an adult is that we have greater choice in nearly every aspect of our lives. Required reading for adults doesn't refer to reading that is assigned; it refers to reading that an adult feels compelled to choose. Although there may be a few texts that warrant the one-text whole-class model, more and more English teachers are incorporating choice into their curriculum. Some teachers use literature circles; others use in-class or out-of-class book clubs. Some teachers offer a choice between paired texts, in which students choose from two texts with similar themes. As we discussed in Chapter 5, this is also a way to include readers of all abilities into mainstream literature discussions if the texts are written at different reading levels. Teachers can also bring students' elective out-of-school readings into the classroom. While this is a regular practice in some advanced classes with "summer reading," it actually has great promise for students of all ability levels. One enterprising teacher I know has her mixed-ability classes complete a reading survey that asks them to identify what themes and issues emerge from some of their elective out-of-school reading. Although she admits that not every student had an example of an outside reading to offer, she builds a thematic unit around one or more of those issues, adding a few core texts of her own.

Multiliteracies and the New Literacies

In this twenty-first century, marked by new technologies and a global explosion of information, adult literacy practices comprise in part what has come to be termed *new literacies* and *multiliteracies*. By *new literacies*, we mean the literacies that have emerged from a multitude of media in a technological society. These can include but are not limited to such literacies as computer literacy, information literacy, media literacy, and visual literacy. These definitions are interconnected and, given the dynamic nature of the technologies that undergird those literacies, these literacies change, thus making it difficult for even the savviest educator to keep up.

What we do know is that until recently, these literacies have not been the subject of formal school study, even though they are the literacies that permeate the literacy landscape of adults. Although a separate volume in this Principles in Practice imprint focuses on technology in the language arts (Sara Kajder's *Adolescents and Digital Literacies: Learning Alongside Our Students*), it is still important to note in this chapter the roles of new literacies in the context of helping adolescents move beyond school-based academic literacy into adult literacy. Because multiple literacies denote literacies that move beyond print or even language-centered modalities, it's important to consider how to acknowledge these literacies with adolescents to help bridge the gap into their multimodal literacy practices as adults, performing as what's been called a "literate citizenship in cyberspace" (Alvermann 22).

Real-World Literacies

Another aspect of adult literacy is the voluntary nature of self-assigned reading. Many researchers have tried to uncover the motivations of readers and to consider how the motivation for out-of-school reading can inform the pedagogical practices for in-school reading. This research has focused on the idea that reading is socially situated. Reading practices are part of adolescents' developing social networks as well as developing social identities. Simply put, as young people's social identities and networks grow and change, so too do their reading choices and affinities.

Adults often read simply for information; we read to find out something we need to know or want to learn about, whether it is about automobiles, travel, cooking, fixing something, gardening, or other hobbies or needs. Adolescents too have a pragmatic streak to their reading. They like to read about the things they are interested in as well as about the things they need to know more about. For example, in their large-scale study of adolescent literacy, Moje and her colleagues discovered that adolescents participate in a wide range of out-of-school reading activities, from informational websites, to books and magazines about their favorite topics, to books or magazine about their own heritage. Moje and her colleagues concluded that contrary to popular belief, adolescents even from high poverty settings are "not unmotivated to read" (127). This finding suggests that it is not a general lack of interest in reading that characterizes their lack of engagement with school texts; it might in fact be their response to our curricular choices.

These encouraging statistics about youth reading also suggest that we need to look more closely at the texts offered to young people in school, and at the ways texts are offered . . . rather than simply ascribing low motivation to youth when it comes to reading this type of material. (127)

Somehow, as both the social and intellectual needs of adolescents change, so too must the curriculum of reading. Adolescents need to see the school-based literacy they engage in as part of the flow of adult literacy activity. Not long ago, an adolescent confided to me that on an airplane ride, she was thrilled to see an adult freely reading the same book she was assigned in her English class. She said it made her feel that what she was reading "was not just for high school kids, but something that adults could relate to as well."

To ensure that our adolescents become lifelong readers once they leave the classroom, we need to encourage their out-of-school literacy practices when they are in the classroom. We can do this in a variety of ways. First, we need to ensure that students have a lot of choice in the texts they read in our classroom. Next, we need to recognize that some of adolescents' out-of-school literacy practices have a legitimacy of their own as well as a relevance to their work in school. Although research is promising but not conclusive on the relationship between out-of-school literacies and in-school achievement, many researchers urge teachers to both be aware of and encourage those literacies, despite a completely causal link.

We also need to find some ways to make in-school literacy learning bear some semblance to real-life learning that occurs outside of school. For example, we can bring nonschool texts into the classroom for legitimate study and interpretation. As we discussed in Chapter 3, many real-world texts, such as newspapers, magazine articles, and even websites, can be fruitfully explored in our literature classes. Incorporating such texts into our curriculum serves several purposes. First, it can help young people learn to read and respond to the multiple texts that surround them outside of school. These seductive texts often compete for their attention. As I have argued elsewhere (Appleman, *Critical Encounters*, 2nd ed.), English language arts teachers should help adolescents learn to read and respond to the ideology inscribed in the texts that surround them. Offering students opportunities to help them read the world is one way to extend adolescent literacy into the real-life world of adult literacy.

Another advantage of this approach is that reading and interpreting texts seems to have real-life value. In other words, reading texts that exist outside the sometimes rarified, artificial confines of the classroom—or as Sara Kadjer has called it, bringing the outside in—can also motivate and engage reluctant readers. This includes helping adolescents learn to read and interpret images, whether they be on a television screen, a movie screen, a computer, or even a cell phone. We also can offer more contemporary works of both fiction and nonfiction within the curriculum. We need to think about replacing some of our tried-and-true but now perhaps anachronistic classics, which have become far removed from the realities and rhythms of our students' lives. Research (for example, Moje et al.; Intrator and Kunzman) reports that using more recent and more contemporary works helps improve student motivation and engagement with literature. Many of the issues we have discussed in previous chapters, including issues of gender and access, can be addressed by a more imaginative and inclusive consideration of the texts that should constitute our language arts curriculum.

Ten Things Teachers Can Do to Help Adolescent Readers Become Book-Loving Adults

- Create a parent–teen book club. Invite your teens and their parents to read together.

- Investigate the books on the *New York Times* bestseller list. Offer those books to students as choices.

- Provide powerful examples of adults reading, including yourself. Read with your students sometimes and talk about what you're reading outside of school.

- Consider creating out-of-class book clubs, in which students can read for the pure pleasure of it.

- Offer as much curricular choice as possible. Allow teens to choose what they read.

- Offer shorter pieces of texts to read, including magazines, short-short stories, and articles.

- Rethink your current curricular choices. Remember that students are more likely to read literature that connects to them in some significant way.

- Plan classroom activities as you read that help make the literature become more dynamic.

- Have tons of paperbacks available in your classroom. Haunt garage sales and remainder tables at bookstores.

- If possible, bring in local authors to give book talks to your class. Take field trips to readings where your students can listen to writers discuss literature as a living art.

Conclusion

Our growing concerns about adolescent literacy are really not just limited to adolescent literacy: as parents and teachers we worry that a whole generation of language arts learners may not be growing into the kind of literate adults that we need to sustain a democracy. While no pedagogical technique or literacy initiative, either in or out of the classroom, is sufficient to ameliorate our concerns, it is imperative that we develop our approaches to language learning, both in and out of school, to introduce adolescents to the adult discourses of literacy. As we have seen, research reveals that adolescents do read outside of school and are driven by their social networks, their developing identity, and their own desire to learn. Perhaps if we connect these natural desires to what we do in school, our classrooms will encourage adolescents to become the engaged readers and writers they need to be so that we may thrive as a literate democracy. Perhaps if we create varied literacy opportunities for all of our students, those who seem initially disengaged or on the margins of our classroom will stay in school and not land in prison. My work with those incarcerated students reminds me that our efforts could not be more important or urgent.

In the last chapter, I present some final considerations designed to help us, as literature teachers, consider the importance of a principled practice approach to reading in our classrooms.

**Chapter
Nine**

Reading, Adolescents, and Literature: The Crisis in Context

An Initial Caveat

Throughout this book, we have considered how, as literature teachers, we can address the causes for concern about adolescent literacy as articulated in *Adolescent Literacy: An NCTE Policy Research Brief.* We have considered what it is that we know about adolescent reading, and we have focused on the nature of texts, on gender, on the struggling reader, on assessment, and on ways of fostering adult literacy. If you have this book in your hands, you are most likely a teacher who is professionally active and committed to her students' learning. You probably do the very best you can for all your students nearly every day. So what more can you possibly do to foster the literacy of your secondary students? How can you respond to this cry of concern, to this call for redoubled efforts in light of this literacy crisis?

The largest question facing literature teachers today might be this one: how can we respond to a literacy crisis that is national in scope, complex in its causes, frequently concentrated in specific communities, and rooted in issues that extend well beyond the classroom? We know, for example, that the causes of this crisis are economic, political, cultural, and social. Possible responses to the crisis would appear to rest in other hands. Frankly, many teachers are tired of being told that they have to fix a problem that lies beyond their resources, their authority, and their professional expertise. Then again, a desire to solve such problems is exactly what brought many of us into teaching in the first place.

So, now that we are here, what do we do? As we attempt to define the boundaries of our present literary crisis, we need to bear several things in mind. First, it is not the case that our present teaching practices don't work. They do. In fact, every year substantial expertise and vast resources are committed to the improvement of best practices for the teaching of secondary literature and literacy skills in general. Second, it is not the case that our students are underperforming. It is rather the case that not all students are performing at what's named as appropriate levels. The majority of students in our schools are succeeding. Third, it is not the case that we don't know how to improve education. What we lack is not knowledge but resources, and until conventional resources arrive we must rely on resourcefulness.

The great majority of English language arts teachers work extremely hard to prepare their students for careers, for college, and for life in an increasingly complex world. The vast majority of English language arts teachers are highly skilled and dedicated professionals. The tasks we face vary from community to community, and we need to place ourselves appropriately in the schools that match our abilities and our callings. For some teachers, this means ensuring that all of their students are prepared for success in selective colleges. For others, it means doing everything possible to bring students to high school graduation. The practices and arguments made here in this book are intended to be as generalizable as possible, but all teachers need to enact a curriculum that matches the most immediate needs of their students.

At the end of the day, it may be that there are many things schools cannot rectify, and these factors should be noted at the front end of curricular discussions and professional development activities. Every school and every department must take a developmental approach to literacy education by first discovering what their students can do, what their needs are, and how the school and teachers might meet those needs. Schools cannot, for example, fully remediate years of deficit in language experience among small children, a deficit that some studies (Baker, Simmons, and Kameenui; Nagy; Nelson-Herber) suggest may lie at the heart of the reading crisis. Schools can, on the other hand, make curricular decisions based on the best evidence available in order to increase literacy gains among young people once they are in school.

A New Set of First Principles

To successfully address the present crisis in reading accomplishment, schools and communities need to adopt a series of strategies to create curricula that match their students' needs. It seems highly unlikely that national standards or federal legislation holds the key to literacy improvement. Even worse, it would seem that national standards actually work against good practices in education. For example, such standards create limitations on teacher talents by depriving teachers of the texts and teaching methods that work best for them. In addition, national standards inherently involve standardized testing, which entails a variety of social, ethnic, and economic biases. And the same national standards deny the very real necessity of districts addressing the diversity of student learning needs they face. In general, such standards impoverish curricula by forcing teachers to teach to tests. Our desire to close achievement gaps, while clearly admirable, can actually exacerbate all of these negative trends by increasing an emphasis on drill-and-skill pedagogies—another case of providing the least engaging, least imaginative methods to the students most in need of engagement and imagination.

Even within a single metropolitan area, for example, the disparities can be extreme: in educational needs, financial and human resources, scores on standardized assessments, resource materials, and technology. What constitutes success in one community would be failure in another. For example, in an urban district with a 50 percent dropout rate, the attainment of a 75 percent high school graduation rate would be hailed as a tremendous improvement, whereas in a more affluent suburban district anything less than a 95 percent graduation would be utterly unacceptable. National standards ignore such realities, and in doing so they actually serve to perpetuate the problems at hand.

In addition to diversity of background, local school districts must take into account the aspirations of their students and the families they come from. For some of these students, attending a local state university would be a dream come true, and their schools must support that dream. In a neighboring community, though, students might aspire to Ivy League universities and selective liberal arts colleges. In still other communities, college may be the aspiration of only a few, and while Bill Gates may advocate higher education for everyone, we must be realistic enough in our goals to ensure that our educational reach does not exceed our grasp.

None of this is to say, though, that any student is entitled to less than the best available education, and such an education must ensure preparation of all students for the future. This preparation must include strong literacy skills: an ability not only to read texts but also to interpret them appropriately; an ability to craft messages in a variety of forms and genres to ensure the ability to communicate successfully; and an ability to create meaning from texts of diverse kinds. Literacy education also needs to be interdisciplinary so that it provides access for students to all relevant areas of study. It must prepare students to understand how language works, how it defines our identities, and how it constructs the world in which we live. And finally, it needs to be pedagogically sound, constructed around active practice in a social context that matches that of the communities within which schools operate. To address this set of requirements, I propose the following first principles of literacy and literary instruction.

Select Texts to Fit Student and Community Needs

Perhaps the first question that teachers of literature need to ask concerns what they will teach and why. For decades, the driving principle behind text selection was what E. D. Hirsch called *cultural literacy*, the idea that there are facts and texts with which all citizens should be acquainted. One could concede that Hirsch wanted the right things for the right reasons: a set of cultural associations that would bind us as a nation and a literate society. Given the multiplicity of U.S. society today, however, this goal is nearly impossible. The negotiation alone—as to what should be included in a national cultural canon—would take years, and the implementation would take far longer, all without any guarantee that the goals would be feasible, let alone desirable. The scope of this problem, then, argues that we move in a different direction.

Another idea that we might challenge is the efficacy of dividing literary study into national and historical categories. National literatures and historical periods have long served as the primary organizing principles for literary study, and it is still frequently the case that we arrange our high school curricula in this manner: world literature in the tenth grade, American literature in the eleventh grade, and British literature in the twelfth. Realistically, however, this manner of canonical coverage appears simply to be impossible. In recent years, we have seen colleges and universities exploring other modes of organizing their curricula, and many high schools are doing the same. They are choosing smaller categories of study, including studies in literary genre, theme, and purposes for literature, with each area addressing smaller sets of texts and more identifiable cultural and social circumstances: literatures of war, of family and marriage, the changing nature of tragedy, the bildungsroman, society in conflict, and so on. These thematic and generic links allow students to immerse themselves in literary explorations for shorter periods of time among more interrelated and congruent texts.

In the end, then, our text selections must address student and community needs first and larger cultural interests second. The problem with these cultural concerns is that they are too often abstract, residing at a significant distance from the lives of the students who read about them. Consider Shakespeare for a moment as an eponymous category for everything related to the works of this particular man of genius. Almost no one challenges the cultural value of teaching Shakespeare. But what is Shakespeare to our students, and why should we teach him? Teaching *Romeo and Juliet* within a unit on family and political conflict makes good sense, and by reading it students can identify with the title characters and see how the larger conflicts within a society reach all the way down to people like them. Providing a clear frame for reading, then, is essential if we hope for them to "get it." Text selection, then, should be developmentally appropriate, socially situated, and thematically connected.

Literature Classrooms Should Focus on Skills, Not Knowledge

Suppose a colleague were to say to you, "It doesn't matter what your students read. It only matters that they know what to do with it as they read it." Having considered the question of cultural literacy and perhaps having conceded that it provides a problematic motivation for reading literature, you still find yourself with an objection to your colleague's claim. There is good literature and not-so-good literature, you might respond, and the latter category is a waste of the students' time. This question obviously takes us back to the goals of our curricula. There is a strong argument to be made within our discussion of these goals that what our students can do with literature is more important than what they know about it.

In answer to the question, "What defines a work of literature?" most of us would answer that it must be interpretable: it must convey meaning in a discernable manner, and this meaning must define the purpose of the work. Our primary purpose for teaching literature, then, must be to develop in our students the ability to interpret texts and thereby to construct meaning from cultural artifacts. There is no greater ability for students to develop than the recognition and conscious construction of meaning. To teach literature successfully, then, we must enable students to develop interpretive skills. If they do this well—if they connect emotionally and cognitively with the texts at hand—they will construct knowledge from them.

Gerald Graff reminds us in *Professing Literature* that in the early days of literary study it wasn't even necessary for students to read the texts they studied. They merely had to know who wrote them, when and where, and what they were about. As we think about our favorite works of literature, we surely hope that our students will acquire this knowledge—and with luck an accompanying appreciation. This knowledge should be a secondary or even tertiary concern, since we also want students to use literature as a way of learning about larger social and cultural concerns that will directly affect them.

Literary Instruction Must Make Connections

Since the first and most important goal of studying literature is the construction of meaning, it is important that our curricula provide students with opportunities to make reading meaningful. The primacy of this goal suggests that in teaching literature we should help students form connections with other disciplines and educational concerns. These disciplines can include history, social studies, science, government, and geography, among others. Such interdisciplinary study, besides being symbiotic (in that it enhances student learning in the accompanying discipline), provides contexts and frameworks for constructing literary meaning.

In some cases the associations across disciplines might be obvious. Marjane Satrapi's *Persepolis* gives us a window to explore political unrest, a persistently violent part of the world, and the role of religion in both politics and coming of age. Toni Morrison's *Beloved* offers an opportunity to create interdisciplinary ways of understanding the cruel legacy of slavery. Marge Piercy's "The Secretary Chant" can be an invitation to explore issues of women in the workplace. *Speak* by Laurie Halse Anderson offers a horrific yet all too familiar account of how public conversations about sex and rape actually shape our understanding of what sexual assault is: in this case, a thing to be bridled and suppressed. *The Book Thief* by Markus Zusak offers a fresh lens into the devastation of the Holocaust as well as of death itself. The possibilities for these interdisciplinary associations are seemingly endless, but they would have this in common: they give students the chance to take literature out into the world, and in doing so they can increase their understanding not just of literature but also of the worlds in which it is set.

An even greater opportunity presents itself in the exploration of *meaning*. What do we mean by this term, especially when we talk about constructing meaning from literary reading? Too often we think of meaning as the hidden message, the story beneath the story, or just *the point*, whatever that means to our students. We think of meaning as something with its own essence, as a thing that can reside somewhere within a literary text. These definitions increase the risk that students won't get it, won't understand even what *literary meaning* is. Such definitions keep the mystery of meaning alive. When students come to understand that meaning is an association of numerous concerns that the mind holds to be important—and that each individual mind constructs its own meanings—then the construction of meaning will be less mysterious and easier for them to accomplish.

The Study of Literature Should Also Focus on Issues of Language

Wallace Stevens says in "Adagia" that "language is not the medium of poetry, it is the material of poetry" (171). If he is right, then it is worth our while to look at the material out of which literature is made. Literature provides invaluable opportunities to explore the uses and effects of language, and language not only allows us to name and explore important concepts, but it also disposes us to do so in specific and predictable ways. As Dwight Bollinger said, "Language is not a neutral instrument. It is a thousand ways biased" (68). Thus, to read carefully is to see bias and to recognize its sources as well as its results.

Implicitly, at least, we understand the effect that language can have on people. Ironically, our sensitivities to this function of language often take us in the opposite direction, away from the controversy. Consider, for example, the place of *Adventures of Huckleberry Finn* in today's schools. Mark Twain uses the word *nigger* something like 213 times in the novel. Most of us today are afraid to even write the word, let alone speak it, preferring to refer to it as "the n-word" instead. Clearly, this is a highly controversial topic, but what we miss if we avoid it is a chance to help students understand what the power of this word entails, and maybe why it is that we avoid it so scrupulously. Obscenity, racial and ethnic epithets, slurs concerning sexual preference—none of these categories is "cool for school." And yet they relate closely to issues of media slanting and propaganda, motives of language use that create particular realities reflecting relative truths. These are exactly the uses of language that literate people must be able to recognize. We can teach the idea of connotation, but we must also prepare our students to recognize the emotional wagons that attach themselves to words.

In addition, there are issues of identity that attach themselves to language. Most of us choose to speak in ways that resemble the speech of our communities and the people with whom we identify. At the same time, we single out as different those who do not share our particular language behaviors, the dialects that we speak. It is a well-known principle of sociolinguistics that we prize the language of desirable communities and disparage the language of communities that are less socially valued. While learning about a dialect does not cause us to forego the judgments to which our biases and values give shape, at the very least we should know the source of these judgments, and so should our students. When they read dialect in fiction, for example, they should also hear actual speakers of that dialect, and they should learn about the lives of these people in order that they might construct less biased images of dialect speakers. Literature, as a cultural phenomenon, is a relatively small concern. Language, its varieties, and our judgments about its use are everywhere. The study of literature, then, should focus at some point on language itself, especially on its capacity for constructing realities and on its connection to personal identity.

Literature Education Must Be Active and Socially Situated

Those of us who enjoy the quiet, contemplative nature of reading are perhaps least well-positioned to shape reading programs for young people. Recall that in Chapter 6 we reviewed the resistance that boys have to reading because of its lonely and passive qualities. We need to make literary interpretation an active process: one that can be dramatized, drawn, translated and reenacted, put into our own words, tied to a larger world. Before our students are going to be engaged in processes of reading, they are going to require reading to do something for them. They want reading to provide excitement, to connect with them emotionally, to transport them to places they want to be, and to reflect their lives in recognizable and relevant ways.

One disturbing suggestion is that school-sponsored reading might do the opposite; it might actually drive people away from reading. As *Adolescent Literacy: An NCTE Policy Research Brief* suggests, there is evidence that children who read at early ages eventually stop reading, usually near the beginning of their middle school experience. As James Marshall has noted, this appears to be the time when children either stop reading or take their reading underground. Coincidentally, this is about the time at which school-sponsored reading begins to include "the classics." We recall the often-quoted line from T. S. Eliot—"what we have loved / Others will love; and we will teach them how"—and we attempt to put this desire into practice, typically with less-than-favorable results. At times, at least, we should attempt to discover what *they* might love and teach that, leaving aside for that moment our personal judgments.

To bring students to the engaged and animated reading that we wish them to do, we must situate their reading in social contexts they can recognize and with which they can identify. Of course, it is the job of public schools to prepare students for citizenship, for life in the state that sponsors the school, but we must remember our loyalty to our students as well. As John Dewey said, education needs to fit the school to the child, not the child to the school. If we follow this advice, we should improve student motivation and direction in learning.

Conclusion

While we all acknowledge that there is a literacy crisis in the United States today, we should keep a number of things in mind. First, the discourse around this crisis is political, as are nearly all discourses of crisis. At the same time, though, we can claim that it is well within our grasp to meet the challenges this crisis delivers. Decades of active research in the teaching of reading and literature have yielded clear results and suggested successful directions in which we might move. Among these are several ways to reorient the study of literature. We should bring the outside world into our classrooms. We should make sure that students are actively engaged in fruitful inquiry. We need to help students negotiate meaning in texts on their own terms, and we should do so by ensuring that they are active rather than passive learners.

Rather than attempting to hand down one literary treasure after another to someone who has his arms folded, we should open the metaphorical library. Our choices should not get in our students' way. In addition, we need to look to issues of gender to see where our curricula are misaligned with the socialization of our students. We have colleagues with ample expertise who stand ready to assist us by collaborating in the teaching of content-area knowledge. We have a wealth of knowledge about language and linguistic behaviors that we can share with our students: knowledge they are likely to find fascinating. We need to continue to use classroom assessment techniques to determine for ourselves in our own classrooms what works and what doesn't.

Finally, we need to acknowledge that the current language of crisis conflates two kinds of learners: those who cannot learn—at least not at their present stage of educational development and under their present circumstances—and those who won't learn because they are disengaged, uninterested, or somehow excluded from the curricula we are practicing. Once we acknowledge this distinction, we can act quickly on behalf of one of these two groups. We can more quickly address those students who won't read than those who truly can't. By acting upon this realization, we can reduce the severity of the crisis in a relatively short time, and we can make it easier for others to address the developmental needs of those not yet prepared to learn in a traditional classroom. If the language of crisis impels us to take these steps, it will have proven itself to be a crisis not wasted.

Annotated Bibliography

Books about Research

Christenbury, Leila, Randy Bomer, and Peter Smagorinsky
Handbook of Adolescent Literacy Research.
New York: Guildford Press, 2009. Print.

This handbook is a must for literacy teachers who want to keep current with the most recent trends in literacy research. Compiled by three leading literacy educators, the handbook divides research into three main segments: literacy in school, literacy out of school, and literacy and culture.

Lewis, Cynthia, Patricia Enciso, and Elizabeth Moje, (eds.)
Reframing Sociocultural Research on Literacy: Identity, Agency, and Power.
New York: Routledge, 2007. Print.

This is a terrific resource for teachers who would like to learn more about the sociocultural perspective on reading. An edited volume of collected articles, it includes the perspectives of leading sociocultural researchers and would be particularly helpful for those engaging in teacher research.

Reports

Alliance for Excellent Education
Reading Next: A Vision for Action and Research in Middle and High School Literacy.
New York: Alliance for Excellent Education, 2004. Print.

This report on reading provides some powerful statistics to support the sense of crisis in literacy outlined by *Adolescent Literacy: An NCTE Policy Research Brief*. It then delineates fifteen key elements of adolescent literacy programs including
- Direct, explicit comprehension instruction
- Text-based collaborative learning
- Ongoing summative assessment of students and programs
- Diverse texts, comprehensive and coordinated literacy programs

Learning Point Associates
The National Reading Panel Report: Practical Advice for Teachers.
Naperville, IL: Learning Point Associates, 2006. Print.

Although controversial in its findings and its influence, this report is a must read for those interested in mapping the instructional and ideological landscape of the field of reading. It includes sections on phonics, oral reading fluency, vocabulary, and comprehension strategies. For better or worse, this report has helped shape some of the required components of reading instruction, both at the P-12 level and in teacher education.

National Endowment for the Arts
To Read or Not to Read: A Question of National Consequence.
Washington, DC: National Endowment for the Arts, 2007. Print.

Unlike the previous reports cited, this report does not offer specific, programmatic fixes. Rather, it is designed to "initiate a serious discussion" about the level of literacy in the United States by providing a snapshot of the reading patterns and habits of a cross-section of Americans, including schoolchildren.

Teacher Resources

Beers, Kylene, Robert Probst, and Linda Rief
Adolescent Literacy: Turning Promise into Practice.
Portsmouth, NH: Heinemann, 2007. Print.

This is a lively and accessible collection of advice about literacy in general and, in many cases, reading in particular, from twenty-five "literacy leaders" who approach adolescent literacy from the perspectives of classroom teachers, literacy researchers, and English educators.

Gallagher, Kelly
Readicide: How Schools Are Killing Reading and What You Can Do about It.
Stenhouse, 2009. Print.

This book considers that constellation of factors that have led to the documented decline in reading for pleasure. Gallagher points to the influence of standardized tests, mandated curricula, and some of the practices in standard literature instruction. It's an inspiring call to rethink our instructional paradigms when it comes to teaching literature.

Miller, Donalyn
The Book Whisperer.
Hoboken, NJ: John Wiley & Sons, 2009. Print.

Donalyn Miller writes a regular column for *Teacher Magazine*, and she's compiled some of her best ideas for encouraging young people to read in this accessible and engaging book. This book is particularly useful for middle school teachers seeking specific strategies and book suggestions for reluctant readers.

Olson, Carol Booth
The Reading/Writing Connection: Strategies for Teaching and Learning in the Secondary Classroom (2nd ed.)
Columbus, OH: Allyn & Bacon, 2006. Print.

This very useful book offers specific strategies for the literature teacher in both middle and high school levels. Olson offers accessible descriptions of the cognitive processes that underlie reading and offers ways to help those processes become visible to one's students. As the name of the book suggests, she also offers ways to integrate reading and writing instruction.

Smith, Michael W., and Jeffrey D. Wilhelm
"Reading Don't Fix No Chevys": Literacy in the Lives of Young Men.
Portsmouth, NH: Heinemann, 2007. Print.

This important book bridges the research/resource divide in that it provides powerful and current research on boys and reading and, at the same time, specific lessons for teachers that emerge from the research. Anyone interested in learning more about boys and reading, which should, of course, be all of us, needs to have this book.

Other

Pennac, Daniel
The Secrets of Reading: Better Than Life
Toronto, Canada: Coach House Press, 1994. Print.

A lovely little book that is neither research nor resource. It is simply a beautiful meditation on why it is that we read and why we must encourage our children to become readers.

Works Cited

Alvermann, Donna E. "Sociocultural Constructions of Adolescence and Young People's Literacies." Christenbury, Bomer, and Smagorinsky 14–28.

Alvermann, Donna E., and Amy Alexandra Wilson. "Redefining Adolescent Literacy Instruction." *Literacy for the New Millennium.* Vol. 3. Ed. Barbara J. Guzzetti. Westport, CT: Praeger, 2007. Print. 3–20.

Applebee, Arthur N. *Literature in the Secondary School: Studies of Curriculum and Instruction in the United States.* Urbana, IL: NCTE, 1993. Print. NCTE Research Report No. 25.

Appleman, Deborah. *Critical Encounters in High School English: Teaching Literary Theory to Adolescents.* New York: Teachers College; Urbana, IL, NCTE, 2000. Print.

———. *Critical Encounters in High School English: Teaching Literary Theory to Adolescents.* 2nd ed. New York: Teachers College; Urbana, IL: NCTE, 2009. Print.

———. *Reading for Themselves: How to Transform Adolescents into Lifelong Readers through Out-of-Class Book Clubs.* Portsmouth, NH: Heinemann, 2006. Print.

Appleman, Deborah, and Michael F. Graves. *Scaffolding Adolescents' Experiences with Literature.* 2010. (Under submission).

Appleman, Deborah, and John Schmit. "Literary Theory behind Bars: Exploring Critical Practices in a Prison Setting." NCTE Annual Convention. Marriott Marquis Times Square, New York. 16 Nov. 2007. Address.

Atwell, Nancie. *In the Middle: New Understandings about Writing, Reading, and Learning.* Portsmouth, NH: Heinemann, 1998. Print.

———. *The Reading Zone: How to Help Kids become Skilled, Passionate, Habitual, Critical Readers.* New York: Scholastic, 2007. Print.

Baker, Scott K., Deborah C. Simmons, and Edward J. Kameenui. *Vocabulary Acquisition: Curricular and Instructional Implications for Diverse Learners.* Eugene, OR: National Center to Improve the Tools of Educators, 1995. Print. Technical Report No. 14.

Beach, Richard, and Jamie Myers. *Inquiry-Based English Instruction: Engaging Students in Life and Literature.* New York: Teachers College, 2001. Print.

Beers, Kylene. *When Kids Can't Read: What Teachers Can Do: A Guide for Teachers 6–12.* Portsmouth, NH: Heinemann, 2003. Print.

Biancarosa, Gina, and Catherine E. Snow. *Reading Next—A Vision for Action and Research in Middle and High School Literacy: A Report from Carnegie Corporation of New York.* Washington, DC: Alliance for Excellent Education, 2004. Print.

Bollinger, Dwight. *Language, the Loaded Weapon: The Use and Abuse of Language Today.* New York: Longman, 1980. Print.

Butler, Judith. *Gender Trouble: Feminism and the Subversion of Identity.* New York: Routledge, 1990. Print.

Chomsky, Noam, and George A. Miller. "Introduction to the Formal Analysis of Natural Languages." *Handbook of Mathematical Psychology.* Ed. R. D. Luce, R. B. Bush, and E. Galanter. New York/London: Wiley & Sons, 1963. Print.

Christenbury, Leila, Randy Bomer, and Peter Smagorinsky, eds. *Handbook of Adolescent Literacy Research.* New York: Guilford Press, 2009. Print.

Cisneros, Sandra. *The House on Mango Street.* New York: Vintage Books, 1991. Print.

Compton-Lilly, Catherine. *Breaking the Silence: Recognizing the Social and Cultural Resources Students Bring to the Classroom.* Newark, DE: IRA, 2009. Print.

Conley, Mark W. "Cognitive Strategy Instruction for Adolescents: What We Know about the Promise, What We Don't Know about the Potential." *Harvard Educational Review* 78.1 (2008): 84–106. Print.

Conners, Sean. "Graphic Young Adult Novels: Deconstructing and (Re) Interpreting Persepolis from a Cultural Critical Perspective." *Interpretive Play: Using Critical Perspectives to Teach Young Adult Literature.* Ed. Anna O. Soter, Mark Faust, and Theresa Rogers. Norwood, MA: Christopher-Gordon, 2008. 179–90. Print.

Csikszentmihalyi, Mihaly. *Beyond Boredom and Anxiety: Experiencing Flow in Work and Play.* San Francisco: Jossey-Bass, 1975. Print.

Elley, Warwick B. *How in the World Do Students Read? IEA Study of Reading Literacy.* The Hague, Netherlands: International Association for the Evaluation of Educational Achievement, 1992. Print.

Fairclough, Norman. *Language and Power.* London: Longman, 1989. Print.

Fisher, Maisha T. *Writing in Rhythm: Spoken Word Poetry in Urban Classrooms.* New York: Teachers College, 2006. Print.

Gallagher, Kelly. *Readicide: How Schools Are Killing Reading and What You Can Do about It.* Portland, ME: Stenhouse, 2009. Print.

Gee, James Paul. *Social Linguistics and Literacies: Ideology in Discourses.* 3rd ed. New York: Routledge, 2008. Print.

———. *What Video Games Have to Teach Us about Learning and Literacy.* New York: Palgrave Macmillan, 2003. Print.

Goodman, Kenneth S. "A Linguistic Study of Cues and Miscues in Reading." *Elementary English* 42.6 (1965): 639–43. Print.

Graff, Gerald. *Professing Literature: An Institutional History.* Chicago: U of Chicago P, 1989. Print.

Graves, Michael F., and Bonnie B. Graves. *Scaffolding Reading Experiences: Designs for Student Success.* 2nd ed. Norwood, MA: Christopher-Gordon, 2003. Print.

Greene, Stuart, ed. *Literacy as a Civil Right: Reclaiming Social Justice in Literacy Teaching and Learning.* New York: Lang, 2008. Print.

Guzzetti, Barbara J. "Lessons on Literacy Learning and Teaching: Listening to Adolescent Girls." Christenbury, Bomer, and Smagoroinsky 372–85.

Hirsch, E. D., Joseph F. Kett, and James S. Trefil. *Cultural Literacy: What Every American Needs to Know.* Boston: Houghton Mifflin, 1987. Print.

Hull, Glynda, and Katherine Schultz. "Literacy and Learning Out of School: A Review of Theory and Research." *Review of Educational Research* 71.4 (2001): 575–611. Print.

Hynds, Susan, and Deborah Appleman. "Walking our Talk: Between Response and Responsibility in the Literature Classroom." *English Education* 29.4 (1997): 272–94 Print.

Intrator, Sam M., and Robert Kunzman. "Who Are Adolescents Today?: Youth Voices and What They Tell Us." Christenbury, Bomer, and Smagoroinsky 29–45.

Jacobs, Vicki A. "Adolescent Literacy: Putting the Crisis in Context." *Harvard Educational Review* 78.1 (2008): 7–39. Print.

Jago, Carol. *Classics in the Classroom: Designing Accessible Literature Lessons.* Portsmouth, NH: Heinemann, 2004. Print.

Jarrell, Randall. *The Death of the Ball Turret Gunner: A Poem.* New York: D. Lewis, 1969. Print.

Johannessen, Larry R., and Thomas M. McCann. "Adolescents Who Struggle with Literacy." Christenbury, Bomer, and Smagoroinsky 65–79.

Kajder, Sara B. *Bringing the Outside In: Visual Ways to Engage Reluctant Readers.* Portland, ME: Stenhouse, 2006. Print.

———. *Adolescents and Digital Literacies: Learning Alongside Our Students.* Urbana, IL: NCTE, 2010. Print.

Kamil, Michael L., Geoffrey D. Borman, Janice Dole, Cathleen C. Kral, Terry Salinger, and Joseph Torgesen. *Improving Adolescent Literacy: Effective Classroom and Intervention Practices.* Washington, DC: National Center for Education Evaluation and Regional Assistance, Institute of Education Sciences, U.S. Department of Education, 2008. Print.

Kindlon, Dan, Michael Thompson, and Teresa Barker. *Raising Cain: Protecting the Emotional Life of Boys.* New York: Ballantine, 1999. Print.

Knight, Mike. "The Mystery of the Struggling Reader." *Mpls. St. Paul Magazine,* Sept. 2008. Web. http://www.mspmag.com/education/raisingreaders/raisingreaderssept08/112808.asp.>

Lakoff, George. *Women, Fire, and Dangerous Things: What Categories Reveal about the Mind.* Chicago: University of Chicago Press, 1987. Print.

Landsman, Julie. *A White Teacher Talks about Race.* Lanham, MD: Rowman, 2009. Print.

Langer, Judith A. *Envisioning Literature: Literary Understanding and Literature Instruction.* New York: Teachers College, 1995. Print.

Lee, Carol D. *Culture, Literacy, and Learning: Taking Bloom in the Midst of the Whirlwind.* New York: Teachers College, 2007. Print.

Lee, Jihyun, Wendy S. Grigg, and Patricia L. Donahue. *The Nation's Report Card: Reading 2007.* Washington, DC: National Center for Education Statistics, Institute of Education Sciences, U.S. Department of Education, 2007. Print.

Lewis, Cynthia, Patricia Enciso, and Elizabeth Birr Moje, eds. *Reframing Sociocultural Research on Literacy: Identity, Agency, and Power.* Mahwah, NJ: Erlbaum, 2007. Print.

Mahar, Donna. "Positioning in Middle School Culture: Gender, Race, Social Class, and Power." *Journal of Adolescent & Adult Literacy* 45.3 (2001): 200–09. Print.

Mahiri, Jabari. *What They Don't Learn in School: Literacy in the Lives of Urban Youth.* Vol. 1. New York: Peter Lang, 2004. Print.

Marshall, James D. "Reconstructing the Literature Classroom: Teaching Texts in a New Century." NCTE Second International Conference. Heidelberg, Germany. 13 Aug. 1996. Address.

Martino, Wayne. "Mucking Around in Class, Giving Crap, and Acting Cool: Adolescent Boys Enacting Masculinities at School." *Canadian Journal of Education* 25.2 (2000):102–12. Print.

Mediascope. *Popular Culture and the American Child.* Issue Brief. *Mediascope.org.* Mediascope, 2005. Print.

Moje, Elizabeth Birr, Melanie Overby, Nicole Tysvaer, and Karen Morris. "The Complex World of Adolescent Literacy: Myths, Motivations, and Mysteries." *Harvard Educational Review* 78.1 (2008): 107–54. Print.

Moll, Luis C., and James B. Greenberg. "Creating Zones of Possibilities: Combining Social Contexts for Instruction." *Vygotsky and Education: Instructional Implications and Applications of Sociohistorical Psychology.* Ed. Luis C. Moll. New York: Cambridge UP, 1990. 319–48. Print.

Monahan, Pat. "You Want *Me* to Teach Reading? Confessions of a Secondary Literature Teacher." *English Journal* 97.6 (2008): 98–104. Print.

Morrell, Ernest. *Linking Literacy and Popular Culture: Finding Connections for Lifelong Learning.* Norwood, MA: Christopher-Gordon, 2004. Print.

Nagy, William E. *Teaching Vocabulary to Improve Reading Comprehension.* Urbana, IL: ERIC/RCS and NCTE; Newark, DE: IRA, 1988. Print.

National Center for Education Statistics. *The Nation's Report Card: Reading 2007.* Washington, DC: NCES, Sept. 2007. Print. Report No. NCES2007496.

National Endowment for the Arts. *Reading at Risk: A Survey of Literary Reading in America.* Washington, DC: NEA, July 2004. Print. Report No 46.

———. *To Read or Not to Read: A Question of National Consequence.* Washington, DC: NEA, Nov. 2007. Print. Research Report No. 47.

Nelson-Herber, Joan. "Expanding and Refining Vocabulary in Content Areas." *Journal of Reading* 29.7 (1986): 626–33. Print.

Newkirk, Thomas. *Misreading Masculinity: Boys, Literacy, and Popular Culture.* Portsmouth, NH: Heinemann, 2002. Print.

O'Brien, David, Roger Stewart, and Richard Beach. "Proficient Reading in School: Traditional Paradigms and New Textual Landscapes." Christenbury, Bomer, and Smagorinsky 80–97.

Ogbu, John U. *Black American Students in an Affluent Suburb: A Study of Academic Disengagement.* Mahwah, NJ: Erlbaum, 2003. Print.

Olson, Carol Booth. *The Reading/Writing Connection: Strategies for Teaching and Learning in the Secondary Classroom.* Boston: Allyn and Bacon, 2006. Print.

Pirie, Bruce. *Teenage Boys and High School English.* Portsmouth, NH: Heinemann, 2002. Print.

Rosch, Eleanor. *Basic Objects in Natural Categories.* Berkeley: Language Behavior Research Laboratory, University of California, 1975. Print.

Rosenblatt, Louise M. *The Reader, the Text, the Poem: The Transactional Theory of the Literary Work.* Carbondale, IL: Southern Illinois University Press, 1978. Print.

Satrapi, Marjane. *Persepolis.* New York: Pantheon Books, 2003. Print.

Saussure, Ferdinand de. *Course in General Linguistics.* New York: Philosophical Library, 1959. Print.

Schoenbach, Ruth, Cynthia Greenleaf, Christine Cziko, and Lori Hurwitz. *Reading for Understanding: A Guide to Improving Reading in Middle and High School Classrooms.* San Francisco: Jossey-Bass, 1999. Print.

Shanahan, Timothy. "Research-Based Reading Instruction: Myths about the National Reading Panel Report." *The*

Reading Teacher 56.7 (2003): 646–55. Print.

Smith, Frank. *Reading without Nonsense*. 3rd ed. New York: Teachers College, 1997. Print.

Smith, Michael W., and Jeffrey D. Wilhelm. "Boys and Literacy: Complexity and Multiplicity." Christenbury, Bomer, and Smagorinsky 360–71.

———. *"Reading Don't Fix No Chevys": Literacy in the Lives of Young Men*. Portsmouth, NH: Heinemann, 2002. Print.

Smith, Sally A. "Talking about 'Real Stuff': Explorations of Agency and Romance in an All-Girls' Book Club." *Language Arts* 78.1 (2000): 30–38. Print.

Smydo, Joe. "End of the Reading Wars: Phonics vs. Whole-Word Battle Gives Way to What's Best for Child." *Pittsburgh Post-Gazette* 26 Aug. 2007. Web. 24 Feb. 2010.

Stevens, Wallace. *Opus Posthumous*. New York: Knopf, 1957. Print.

Street, Brian V. *Social Literacies: Critical Approaches to Literacy in Development, Ethnography, and Education*. New York: Longman, 1995. Print.

Tannen, Deborah. *You Just Don't Understand: Women and Men in Conversation*. New York: Ballantine, 1991. Print.

Tatum, Alfred W. *Reading for Their Life: (Re)Building the Textual Lineages of African American Adolescent Males*. Portsmouth, NH: Heinemann, 2009. Print.

———. *Teaching Reading to Black Adolescent Males: Closing the Achievement Gap*. Portland, ME: Stenhouse, 2005. Print.

Thompson, Gail L. *Through Ebony Eyes: What Teachers Need to Know but Are Afraid to Ask about African American Students*. San Francisco: Jossey-Bass, 2007. Print.

United Nations Educational, Scientific and Cultural Organization. *The Plurality of Literacy and its Implications for Policies and Programmes*. Paris: UNESCO, 2004. Web. 24 Feb. 2010.

Wilhelm, Jeffrey D. *Action Strategies for Deepening Comprehension: Role Plays, Text Structure Tableaux, Talking Statues, and Other Enactment Techniques That Engage Students with Text*. New York: Scholastic, 2002. Print.

———. *Improving Comprehension with Think-Aloud Strategies*. New York: Scholastic, 2001. Print.

———. *"You Gotta BE the Book": Teaching Engaged and Reflective Reading with Adolescents*. New York: Teachers College, 1997. Print.

Wilhelm, Jeffrey D., and Michael W. Smith. "Making It Matter through the Power of Inquiry." *Adolescent Literacy: Turning Promise into Practice*. Ed. Kylene Beers, Robert E. Probst, and Linda Rief. Portsmouth, NH: Heinemann, 2007. 231–42. Print.

Yancy, Kathleen Blake. *Teaching Literature as Reflective Practice*. Urbana, IL: NCTE, 2004. Print.

Index

Author

 Deborah Appleman is the Hollis L. Caswell professor and chair of educational studies and director of the Summer Writing Program at Carleton College. Appleman's recent research has focused on teaching college-level language and literature courses at the Minnesota Correctional Facility–Stillwater for inmates who are interested in pursuing postsecondary education.

Appleman taught high school English for nine years before receiving her doctorate in 1986 from the University of Minnesota. At Carleton she teaches educational psychology, teenage wasteland, issues in urban education, introduction to American studies, and methods of literacy instruction. She also was a visiting professor at Syracuse University and at the University of California, Berkeley.

Appleman's primary research interests include adolescent response to literature, teaching literary theory to secondary students, and adolescent response to poetry. Her most recent book, *From the Inside Out: Letters to Young Men and Other Writings—Poetry and Prose from Prison* features the creative work of incarcerated writers. She also authored *Reading for Themselves: How to Transform Adolescents into Lifelong Readers through Out-of-Class Book Clubs.* She is the coauthor of *Teaching Literature to Adolescents* with Richard Beach, Susan Hynds, and Jeffrey Wilhelm. Her book *Critical Encounters in High School English: Teaching Literary Theory to Adolescents,* now in its second edition, was published jointly by Teachers College Press and the National Council of Teachers of English and is widely used in methods classes across the country. Appleman also has written numerous book chapters and articles on adolescent response to literature and coedited *Braided Lives,* a multicultural literature anthology published by the Minnesota Humanities Commission. She has presented many papers at professional conferences for the American Educational Research Association, the National Council of Teachers of English, the Assembly of Research of NCTE, and the National Reading Conference as well as at international conferences in Germany, England, France, and Australia. She has worked with teachers across the country, conducting workshops in California, Maine, Nebraska, Oregon, Washington, Wisconsin, Illinois, Iowa, New York, and Minnesota. She has also worked with teachers in Australia and Japan.

Appleman served as co-chair of NCTE's Commission on English and English Studies, president of the Minnesota Council of Teachers of English, co-chair of the Assembly of Research, co-chair of AERA's literature SIG, and the executive committee of NCTE's Conference on English Education. She currently serves on NCTE Standing Committee on Research.

This book was typeset in Jansen Text and BotonBQ by
Barbara Frazier.

Typefaces used on the cover include American Typewriter,
Frutiger Bold, Formata Light, and Formata Bold.

The book was printed on 60-lb Williamsburg Recycled Offset
paper by Versa Press, Inc.